BT
2.25

D0941327

WORDSWORTH

and the

Literature of Travel

WORDSWORTH
and the
Literature of Travel

by

CHARLES NORTON COE

Associate Professor of English
The University of Idaho

BOOKMAN ASSOCIATES : NEW YORK

To My
MOTHER AND FATHER

ACKNOWLEDGEMENTS

THE SUGGESTION THAT A THOROUGH INVESTIGATION OF WORDS-worth's reading in travel books might make a worthwhile contribution to Wordsworthian scholarship was first made to me by Dr. J. Bard McNulty, Assistant Professor of English at Trinity College. The subject was originally a doctoral dissertation at the Yale Graduate School under the direction of Dr. Frederick A. Pottle, Sterling Professor of English. To both of these scholars I am deeply grateful for their many helpful suggestions. Thanks are also due to Drs. Raymond D. Havens and Don Cameron Allen, editors of *Modern Language Notes,* for their assistance in connection with several of my articles on this subject published in that journal, as well as for the suggestion that the subject should be treated at greater length. I wish also to acknowledge my gratitude to the Editor of *Notes and Queries* for his helpful criticism of my articles published in that journal. And to the publishers of these two journals, the Johns Hopkins Press and the Oxford University Press, I wish to acknowledge thanks for their generosity in allowing me to include these articles in the present study.

For permission to quote from copyrighted material I am grateful to the following publishers: Jonathan Cape, Ltd., London, for Hugh I'Anson Fausset, *The Lost Leader: A Study of Wordsworth,* 1933. The Champlain Society, Toronto, for Samuel Hearne, *Journal from Hudson's Bay to the Northern Ocean,* ed. J. B. Tyrrell, 1911. The Clarendon Press, Oxford, for *Wordsworth's Prelude,* ed. Ernest de Selincourt, 1926; *The Letters of William and Dorothy Wordsworth,* ed. Ernest de Selincourt. 6 vols., 1935-39; *The Poetical Works of William Wordsworth,* ed. Ernest de Selincourt and Helen Darbishire. 5 vols., 1940-49. Columbia University

Press, New York, for Hoxie Neale Fairchild, *The Noble Savage: a Study in Romantic Naturalism,* 1928. E. P. Dutton and Company, New York, for Emile Legouis, *The Early Life of William Wordsworth,* translated by J. W. Matthews, 1932. Ginn and Company, Boston, for Lane Cooper, *Methods and Aims in the Study of Literature,* 1915. Harcourt, Brace and Company, New York, for René Wellek and Austin Warren, *Theory of Literature,* 1948. The Johns Hopkins Press, Baltimore, for Nathan Bryllion Fagin, *William Bartram: Interpreter of the American Landscape,* 1933; Raymond D. Havens, *The Mind of a Poet,* 1941; Arthur O. Lovejoy and George Boas, *A Documentary History of Primitivism and Related Ideas,* 1935. The Macmillan Company, New York, for *The Journals of Dorothy Wordsworth,* ed. Ernest de Selincourt. 2 vols., 1941. The Odyssey Press, New York, for *Wordsworth: Representative Poems,* ed. Arthur Beatty, 1937.

I am also indebted to Miss Jean Buchert of the Yale Graduate School and to Professor McNulty for their kind assistance in reading proof.

Finally, I wish to acknowledge my gratitude to the Regents and Administration of the University of Idaho for their generous grant of a year's leave of absence to revise and publish this book.

New Haven, Connecticut, October, 1952.   C.N.C.

TABLE OF CONTENTS

INTRODUCTION: History and Scope of the Subject

IN HIS ESSAY, "A GLANCE AT WORDSWORTH'S READING," PROFESSOR Lane Cooper takes the critics to task for insisting that Wordsworth was not widely read and that his poetry was not influenced by books. Beginning with Emerson's remark that Wordsworth had "no master but nature and solitude," Cooper traces the opinions of several critics which tend to give a false picture of Wordsworth's preparation for the poet's calling and his method of composing. He summarizes the still popular view as follows:

> To his average acquaintance Wordsworth is a comforting type of poet; in order to appreciate him, it would seem, one does not need to know very much . . . the poet of Rydal Mount is a great non-reading seer of 'nature,' uninfluenced by books and neglectful of bookish lore, a genius who in a peculiar sense may be contemplated apart, and fully understood without recourse to conventional and irksome scholarly helps. . . . [to account for this attitude toward Wordsworth, he adds,] there is the usual reluctance of the uninitiated to credit any genius with the need of external assistance in his work, and an allied indolent reluctance of half-initiated criticasters to grant that studying his 'sources'—the books that he 'devoured, or studiously perused'—will ever aid us in understanding a seer; as if we did not need a poet's education in order to look with a poet's eyes.[1]

Professor Cooper might have mentioned as typical views of Wordsworth's reading the following statements by two of the poet's most distinguished biographers, Legouis and Harper: "Wordsworth gives us the impression that, had he lived alone on a bookless earth, he would have reached the same conclusions";[2] "few other great poets are so little indebted to books."[3]

The assumption that Wordsworth's poetry was not influenced

by books is frequently controverted, both by the poet's own remarks and by the findings of scholars who have investigated his reading. It has been recognized for some time, at least by specialists in the field, that he borrowed from travel books. Besides Cooper's essay cited above, other scholars have dealt with this matter. In his introduction to the variorum edition of *The Prelude,* de Selincourt writes:

> The servant-maid at Rydal Mount, who told a visitor that her master's study was in the fields, touched unquestionably upon the main source of his inspiration, but her pretty epigram did not comprise the whole truth of the matter; and the poet who spoke of books as 'Powers only less than Nature's self, which is the breath of God,' was not likely to neglect them. Yet the superficial critic has always tended to under-rate their influence upon him. . . . He had at all times a passion for the literature of travel, and insisted on its value in widening his outlook and enriching his experience.[4]

In *The Mind of a Poet* Professor Havens lists a dozen or more references under the heading, "Wordsworth's fondness for books of travel." Kurt Lienemann, in his dissertation, *Die Belesenheit von William Wordsworth,* includes a few pages on travel books. And there have been treatments of this subject by Lowes, Legouis, and others. In spite of this, the popular concept of Wordsworth working independently of books seem to endure; and as recently as 1933, T. S. Eliot spoke of Wordsworth as "indifferent to books."[5]

In view of the persistence of these superficial and sentimental notions, this study proposes to examine Wordsworth's reading in travel books to clear up certain misconceptions regarding his method of composing and to show the full extent to which reading in the literature of travel influenced the poet whose indifference to books has been so long proclaimed.

To indicate the importance of Wordsworth's reading, it may be helpful to point out that, with him, travel and reading travel books often went hand in hand with writing poetry. Consider, for instance, the number of his poems associated with walking tours or trips. First of all, there is *An Evening Walk*. There is also *Descriptive Sketches* which celebrates a tour made with Robert Jones in 1790; some details of the same tour are recounted in the sixth book of *The Prelude*. Then there are the four memorials of his later tours: in Scotland in 1803, and again in 1814; on the continent in 1820; in Italy in 1837. There is *Yarrow Revisited . . . composed . . . during a tour in Scotland*. There is also the *Poems composed or suggested during a tour, in the summer of 1833*. When we think of Wordsworth's shorter poems, the *Lines composed a few miles above Tintern Abbey* comes to mind at once as the most famous of many short poems occasioned by a trip. And as this study progresses, it will be shown that Wordsworth read and borrowed from travel books relating to all the countries that he toured and celebrated in verse.

Let us consider first some of Wordsworth's general statements regarding travel books. Two references dating from his boyhood years reveal an interest in this type of reading. In the *Autobiographical Memoranda,* he says: "Of my earliest days at school I have little to say, but that they were very happy ones, chiefly because I was left at liberty, then and in the vacations, to read whatever books I liked. For example, I read . . . Gulliver's Travels." [6] And among the cherished treasures of his boyhood, he mentions a romanticized account of travel and adventure, *The Arabian Nights*. Referring in *The Prelude* to his school days at Hawkshead, he tells us:

> I had a precious treasure at that time
> A little, yellow canvas-cover'd Book,
> A slender abstract of the Arabian Tales.[7]
>
> (V, 482-4, 1805)

Statements referring to a slightly later period in his life reveal an interest in the type of travel book from which he was already beginning to borrow ideas and phrases for his poems; for example, in 1796 he is concerned about the loss of two books that had been lent from his library. Writing to William Mathews on March 21, he says: "I hope you have preserved the catalogue of my books left at Montagu's . . . Gilpin's tour into Scotland, and his northern tour, each 2 vols., ought to be amongst the number." [8] Two years later he gives a hint as to the importance he attached to reading travel books in preparation for writing poetry. The following excerpt is from a letter of March 6, 1798 to James Tobin: "If you could collect for me any books of travels you would render me an essential service, as without much of such reading my present labours [i.e., work on *The Recluse*] cannot be brought to a conclusion." [9] In the Fenwick note to *The Complaint of a Forsaken Indian Woman,* he remarks: "Written at Alfoxden in 1798, where I read Hearne's Journey with deep interest." [10] By 1812 Wordsworth had become so engrossed in reading travel books that he wrote to Francis Wrangham, "The only *modern* Books that I read are those of travels, or such as relate to matters of fact." [11]

Fortunately, too, Wordsworth acknowledged some of his borrowings from books of travel. There are more than twenty such acknowledgements to be found, mainly among his own notes to the poems. Before considering them, however, let us examine the poet's lifelong interest in travel which is obviously related to his interest in travel books.

Although Wordsworth's visit to London while he was a student at Cambridge served mainly to reenforce his preference for country over city life, as a boy at Hawkshead he thought of a trip to the city as surpassing even the most exciting adventures and journeys into distant lands. In the seventh book of *The Prelude* he mentions this feeling and speaks of the envy he felt toward one of his companions who had made the trip to London:

There was a time when whatsoe'er is feigned

> Of airy palaces, and gardens built
> By Genii of romance; or hath in grave
> Authentic history been set forth of Rome,
> Alcairo, Babylon, or Persepolis;
> Or given upon report by Pilgrim friars,
> Of golden cities ten months' journey deep
> Among Tartarian wilds — fell short, far short,
> Of what my fond simplicity believed
> And thought of London. . . .
> > in our flock of boys
> Was One, a cripple from his birth, whom chance
> Summoned from school to London; fortunate
> And envied traveller! (VII, 77-93)

De Selincourt cites this passage as reminiscent of the poet's reading in *Purchas, His Pilgrimes,* a volume of travel books owned by Wordsworth.[12]

Elsewhere in his autobiographical poem Wordsworth speaks of himself as a traveller: "A Traveller I am,/ And all my Tale is of myself," and in the Fenwick note to *The Excursion,* he says that wandering was his "passion." "*Books,* as appears from many passages in [Southey's] writings . . . were in fact *his passion;* and *wandering,* I can with truth affirm, was *mine*." [13] Several of his letters show that this passion for travel, developed at an early age and indulged throughout his life, was still strong in him during his later years. In 1835, writing to Viscount Lowther, he remarks: "I have an ardent desire to be at liberty . . . to travel a little on the Continent—in Italy especially." A year later, in a letter to William Rowan Hamilton, Wordsworth writes: "How should I like, old as I am, to visit those classic shores, and the Holy Land, with all its remembrances, so sweet and solemn!" [14] He has this to say about his Italian tour in 1837: "During my whole life I had felt a strong desire to visit Rome and the other celebrated cities and regions of Italy. . . . My excellent friend H. C. Robinson readily consented to accompany me, and in March, 1837, we set off from London." [15]

Though Wordsworth insisted that his passion for travel had been "counteracted by inability from want of fortune to fulfill my wishes," [16] he managed, nevertheless, to tour England, Scotland, Wales, Ireland, Holland, France, Germany, Switzerland, and Italy. The fact that he travelled in these countries complicates the problem of establishing accurately his indebtedness to travel books, even though we know that he read many accounts of tours through all the above-mentioned places. One still has to distinguish between what his poetry owes to first-hand observation and what is borrowed from the accounts of earlier travelers. In helping us make this distinction, his own notes, which mention specifically many of his borrowings, are particularly helpful. A complete list of these acknowledgements will be found in the Appendix. Here it will suffice to mention the following: Ramond's translation of Coxe's *Travels in Switzerland,* used extensively in *Descriptive Sketches;* Hearne's *Journey,* and Bartram's *Travels* used in the *Lyrical Ballads;* the travel books of Dampier and Mungo Park, mentioned in notes to *The Prelude;* and Carver's *Travels through North America,* mentioned in *Poems in Two Volumes.* Besides these, there are many other references to travel books found in later poems; in fact as late as 1835 we find Wordsworth making note of his borrowings from travel books in such poems as *The Black Stones of Iona,* and *The Russian Fugitive.*

But a mere listing of Wordsworth's acknowledged borrowings, though it shows something of the extent of his indebtedness to travel books, does not indicate the influence his reading in them had on his poetry. A consideration of this important subject must be left to subsequent chapters, but some light can be shed here on Wordsworth's method of composing. We must return for a moment to the common assumptions alluded to earlier in this chapter: that Wordsworth was not influenced by books, that he would not describe situations or people with which he was not personally familiar, that he would have come to the same conclusions if he had not read any books. It is perfectly clear that many of Wordsworth's own statements lend credence to such generalizations. For example, he frequently talks of having "composed" a poem out-of-doors, extemporaneously. Consider the following typical statements: "Much the greatest part of this poem was composed during my walks upon the banks of the Loire." "Actually composed while I was sitting by the side of the brook that runs down from the Comb." "Nine-tenths of my verses have been murmured out in the open air. . . . One day a stranger . . . asked of one of the female servants . . . permission to see her master's Study. 'This,' said she, leading him forward, 'is my master's library, where he keeps his books; but his study is out of doors.' " "Composed on the road between Nether Stowey and Alfoxden, extempore." "I began it upon leaving Tintern, after crossing the Wye, and concluded it just as I was entering Bristol in the evening, after a ramble of four or five days with my sister. Not a line of it was altered, and not any part of it written down till I reached Bristol." [17]

When we realize that the first poem referred to above was *Descriptive Sketches* and that the last was *Tintern Abbey,* we are forced to ask ourselves just what Wordsworth meant by "composing." We can accept, in the main, the poet's statement that all the details of *Tintern Abbey* were actually formulated in his mind during his tour of the Wye and written down without alteration when he reached Bristol. Nor is this the only poem that Wordsworth says he composed entirely before writing it down. The preamble to his *Prelude* came to him "spontaneously" and was written following his walk along the road from Bristol to Racedown in September, 1795. [18]

> Thus far, O Friend! did I, not used to make
> A present joy the matter of my Song,
> Pour out, that day, my soul in measur'd strains
> *Even in the very words which I have here*
> *Recorded:* to the open fields I told

> A prophecy: *poetic numbers came*
> *Spontaneously.*   (I, 55-61, 1805; italics mine.)

But when Wordsworth speaks of "composing" a much longer poem—*Descriptive Sketches* ran just over 800 lines when originally published — he probably meant that he received his suggestion or inspiration, and even *some* of the details during his various rambles along the banks of the Loire. Henry Crabb Robinson's comment regarding Wordsworth's habit of composing during the Italian tour of 1837 seems to bear out this interpretation. Robinson writes: "I have often been asked whether Mr. W. wrote anything on the journey, and my answer has always been, 'Little or nothing.' Seeds were cast into the earth, and they took root slowly." [19] It is quite possible, of course, that in composing a poem like *Descriptive Sketches,* Wordsworth may have worked at it piecemeal; he could easily have composed 50 or 100 lines per day during his walks, written them down at night, and repeated the performance on the next day. This is not quite the same thing, however, as assuming that such a poem sprang full-grown from the head of the wandering poet; for it suggests some working over and revision during the evening as well as the inevitable changes necessary in fitting the various parts — each, let us say, the result of a day's ramble — into a harmonious whole.

Nor are Wordsworth's own comments on the art of composing all of a piece. In fact, there were times when he criticized other poets, including his favorite, Milton, for minimizing the importance of painstaking labor in the development of poetic style. De Selincourt calls attention to statements in Wordsworth's letters where the poet speaks of some of his poems as:

'effusions rather than compositions, though in justice to myself I must say that upon the correction of the style I have bestowed, as I always do, great labour.' 'The composition of verse,' he wrote later, 'is infinitely more an art than men are prepared to believe, and absolute success in it depends on innumerable *minutiae*. . . . Milton speaks of pouring "easy his unpremeditated verse". It would be harsh, untrue, and odious to say there is anything like cant in this, but it is not *true* to the letter, and tends to mislead.'

De Selincourt goes on to say that Wordsworth's "own description of poetry as 'the spontaneous overflow of powerful feelings' was liable to the same misconstruction. For experience had taught him that this 'spontaneous overflow' was no more than the raw material of art." He concludes with the remark that "Wordsworth's . . . strenuous efforts to gain perfection of form, are seldom sufficiently realized." [20]

That Wordsworth's efforts at composing were sometimes strenuous enough to upset him and probably to worry his sister is brought out in several entries from Dorothy's *Journal* written at Grasmere in the years 1800-1803:

A very fine morning. We walked before Wm. began to work. . . . He was afterwards only partly successful in composition. . . . A very rainy day. Wm. again unsuccessful. . . . Wm. could not compose much, fatigued himself with altering. . . . William working at his poem all the morning. . . . Wm. wrote out part of his poem, and endeavoured to alter it, and so made himself ill.[21]

Actually, one can show that much of Wordsworth's composing, whatever he said about it, and whatever some of his critics have assumed, must have been carried on under less romantic circumstances than is commonly believed. By referring to the poet's own acknowledgements of his borrowings from travel books listed in the Appendix, one can see that Wordsworth sometimes mentioned his use of travel books in the earlier stages of his poetic composition: to supply local color, to recall to his mind the details of a story or incident, or to furnish him with a character. An examination of some of these acknowledgements of indebtedness indicates that, while he was actually writing or revising his poems, he sometimes

19

had a travel book open before him. This examination of his notes and the books to which he refers in them will also prove that, while he was often careful to acknowledge even very slight borrowings, he sometimes forgot about more detailed or significant debts. For example, there are notes to two sonnets (Part II, XXVI and XXIX) in the series, *Poems Dedicated to National Independence and Liberty,* in which Wordsworth acknowledges his debt to Laborde's *View of Spain.* Yet there is a third sonnet in the same series in which the debt to Laborde is closer than in the sonnets noted by Wordsworth. The similarity between the following sonnet and a paragraph from Laborde is obvious.

> In due observance of an ancient rite,
> The rude Biscayans, when their children lie
> Dead in the sinless time of infancy,
> Attire the peaceful corse in vestments white;
> And, in like sign of cloudless triumph bright,
> They bind the unoffending creature's brows
> With happy garlands of the pure white rose:
> Then do a festal company unite
> In choral song; and, while the uplifted cross
> Of Jesus goes before, the child is borne
> Uncovered to his grave: 'tis closed, — her loss
> The Mother *then* mourns, as she needs must mourn;
> But soon, through Christian faith, is grief subdued:
> And joy returns, to brighten fortitude.   (Part II, XXIV)

This is simply a poetic version of the following paragraph from Laborde:

Music, and the appearance of gaiety likewise accompany the funerals of children. When these die before the age of reason, they are carried uncovered to the burial place, dressed in white, with a crown of white roses on their heads; musicians go before, a young chorister carries the cross, and the followers tumultuously proclaim their joy at the happiness of innocence. The mother subdues her grief, resigning herself to heaven. Whatever pain a Biscayan suffers, his faith renders him patient, and he calmly says *Dios lo quiere,* it is God's will.²²

Wordsworth's sonnet contains almost all the details mentioned by Laborde: the corpse clothed in white; white roses bound around the dead child's brow; the chorus of singers; the cross carried in the procession; and the mother's grief subdued through Christian faith. If this were an isolated incident of unacknowledged borrowing, we should have to admit that Wordsworth *might* have remembered all the details in the paragraph from Laborde and might have written the sonnet months or even years after he had read Laborde without recalling his source. That would be unlikely, but possible. Yet when we observe that from this same travel book Wordsworth excerpts a passage which he uses, word for word, as an explanatory note to another sonnet in the same series, we must conclude, either that Wordsworth worked with the book open before him, or that he made detailed notes on his reading. Here is his note to sonnet number XXVI, *The Oak of Guernica*:

> The ancient oak of Guernica, says Laborde in his account of Biscay, is a most venerable natural monument. Ferdinand and Isabella, in the year 1476, after hearing Mass in the church of Santa Maria de la Antigua, repaired to this tree, under which they swore to the Biscayans to maintain their *fueros* (privileges). What other interest belongs to it in the minds of this people will appear from the following.

Except for the last sentence and the supplying of the English equivalent for *fueros,* this note of Wordsworth's is taken *verbatim* from Laborde, II, 345.

On a later occasion Wordsworth again follows word for word the writings of a travel-book author, this time Johann Ebel's *Manuel du Voyageur en Suisse.* In a note to *Desultory Stanzas,* he writes:

> On the 1st of January, 1308, the great day which the confeder-

ated Heroes had chosen for the deliverance of their Country, all the Castles of the Governors were taken by force or stratagem; and the Tyrants themselves conducted, with their Creatures, to the frontiers, after having witnessed the destruction of their Strongholds. From that time the Landenberg has been the place where the Legislators of this division of the Canton assemble.

Though Wordsworth concludes his note by stating that, "the site, which is well described by Ebel, is one of the most beautiful in Switzerland," he gives no indication that in the preceding sentences he has given as his own note, an *exact translation* of Ebel.[23] This is mentioned, not to accuse Wordsworth of plagiarism, but to show that, though some of his borrowings from travel books are admittedly hard to identify because they take the form of vague recollections and subtle echoes, other borrowings are so detailed and exact that they indicate, beyond any doubt, Wordsworth's dependence upon this type of source material in the actual composition of his poems. In fact, one observes that, where Wordsworth acknowledges a borrowing from a travel book, other borrowings can sometimes be found close by. This suggests either a lapse of memory or the possibility that Wordsworth may have noted down only those borrowings that interested him or those that he thought would interest others. While he was not averse to accusing Byron of plagiarism (see his letter to Henry Taylor, December 26, 1823), he apparently did not regard himself as under the same obligation that binds a research student, for example, to acknowledge every borrowing and to indicate the exact extent of his indebtedness.

Enough has been said to indicate that Wordsworth's knowledge of travel books was extensive and his interest in them persistent. Before explaining *how* he used the material found in travel books, we should first consider *why* that type of material interested him. An examination of the relation between Wordsworth's theory of poetry and his reading in travel books should help answer this question.

CHAPTER ONE

TRAVEL BOOKS AND WORDSWORTH'S
THEORY OF POETRY

AN EXAMINATION OF WORDSWORTH'S THEORY OF POETRY MAKES IT
clear that the poet was aware of the advantages of having ideas
suggested to him by the sights he had seen, the people he had
talked with, and the experiences he had undergone. This chapter
will show that, although Wordsworth may not always have been
aware of it, he also benefited greatly from having ideas and words
suggested by his reading. We shall first examine his theory of
poetry and then consider the help he received in his composing by
discovering in his reading of travel books the verbalization of ideas
that must have been loosely suggested by his own experiences. We
shall find that, even in poems which seem to spring entirely from
personal observation, his debt to a particular passage in a travel
book was sometimes very significant.

Wordsworth's theory of poetry can best be analyzed in the
light of his various prefaces and notes, especially the "Preface to
the Second Edition of *Lyrical Ballads*." To begin with, Wordsworth
defines the poet, not as a prophet or seer, but simply as "a man
speaking to men." He elaborates on this basic concept by describing the poet as one "endowed with more lively sensibility, more
enthusiasm and tenderness . . . than are supposed to be common
among mankind." [1] Thus endowed and equipped, the poet can
treat of what Wordsworth regards as the appropriate subject matter for poetry, "the great and universal passions of men, the most
general and interesting of their occupations, and the entire world
of nature." According to Wordsworth the poet should take all time
and space for his province, for "the objects of the Poet's thoughts
are everywhere . . . he will follow wheresoever he can find an

atmosphere of sensation in which to move his wings." Thus the poet "binds together by passion and knowledge the vast empire of human society, as it is spread over the whole earth, and over all time." For Wordsworth this meant, not only detailed and minute observation of the manners and customs of his own neighbors, but travel in foreign lands, as well as wide reading in the books of explorers and adventurers who had observed the customs of many peoples.

For his material Wordsworth preferred "incidents and situations from common life," presented, "as far as was possible in a selection of language really used by men." He wished "at the same time, to throw over them a certain colouring of imagination, whereby ordinary things should be presented to the mind in an unusual aspect; and, further . . . to make these incidents and situations interesting by tracing in them . . . the primary laws of our nature." He chose "humble and rustic life . . . because, in that condition, the essential passions of the heart find a better soil in which they can attain their maturity . . . and speak a plainer and more emphatic language; because in that condition of life our elementary feelings coexist in a state of greater simplicity . . . because the manners of rural life germinate from those elementary feelings . . . and, lastly, because in that condition the passions of men are incorporated with the beautiful and permanent forms of nature."

As for the source of Wordsworth's poetry, we shall later deal more fully with the implications for this study of the important phrase, "emotion recollected in tranquillity," pointing out that between the time of observation and composition there generally came a period of contemplation during which Wordsworth attempted to reduce the multiplicity of his sense impressions to a meaningful image. Here it will suffice to mention that de Selincourt considers "the central point of Wordsworth's creed," the poet's statement "that poetry [takes its origin from] 'emotion recollected in tranquillity,' drawing its inspiration and its material from the great moments of the past, especially from the scenes of childhood and early youth, when feeling is strongest." [2] In *The Prelude* the poet describes his attempt to recall to mind the impressions of his childhood days:

> Oh! mystery of Man, from what a depth
> Proceed thy honours! I am lost, but see
> In simple childhood something of the base
> On which thy greatness stands. . . .
> > The days gone by
> Come back upon me from the dawn almost
> Of life: the hiding-places of my power
> Seem open; I approach, and then they close;
> I see by glimpses now; when age comes on,
> May scarcely see at all, and I would give,
> While yet we may, as far as words can give,
> A substance and a life to what I feel.
> > (XI, 329-41, 1805)

Wordsworth eschews both the subject matter and the style of contemporary poetry, not only because of its "gaudiness and inane phraseology," but for a more basic reason. He regards its subject matter as too abstract and artificial. He prefers to keep his reader "in the company of flesh and blood, persuaded that by so doing I shall interest him."

In order to deal most effectively with his material, Wordsworth explains, "I have at all times endeavoured to look steadily at my subject." In interpreting this statement we should not assume that Wordsworth here advocates objective writing, the accurate reporting of details, or mere descriptive poetry. Note that, in commenting on one of his earliest works, he remarks: "The plan of it [*Evening Walk*] has not been confined to a particular walk or an individual place; *a proof . . . of my unwillingness to submit the poetic spirit to the chains of fact and real circumstance.* The coun-

try is idealized rather than described in any one of its local aspects."
(Italics mine.) Though his poems contain many pictorially accurate
details, his avowed purpose was "to treat of things not as they *are,*
but as they *appear;* not as they exist in themselves, but as they
seem to exist to the *senses,* and to the *passions."* It was not primarily
descriptive ability but the transforming power of the imagination
that interested Wordsworth. This effect he succeeded in communicating in some of his most striking passages of poetry. For example,
he describes the day on which he and Jones crossed the Alps without realizing it as an illustration of "deep and genuine sadness,"
(*Prelude,* VI, 492, 1805). The peasant who informed them of
their error caused "a melancholy slackening" (*Ibid.,* VI, 617) of
their spirits. Yet the most striking part of this passage is not the
descriptive narrative of what happened in 1790, but the lyric
utterance of Wordsworth's recollection of the experience years later
when he was writing that part of *The Prelude* in 1804.[3] For at that
later date he was not concerned with actuality, but with the power
of the imagination to give permanent meaning and significance to
his experience. When the incident occurred he felt sad and melancholy because he had crossed the Alps without knowing it and,
consequently, without experiencing any feeling of exhilaration over
his accomplishment; and also because, now that the objective had
been achieved, he would never have it to look forward to again.
But on recollecting the experience that had at first seemed disappointing, he finds that he has learned from it something about
man's essential nature, something that he can communicate to his
readers to give them pleasure. He has seen that man was made for
continual aspiration and expectation, and therefore has no need
for the outward symbols of accomplishment.

> Imagination — here the Power so called
> Through sad incompetence of human speech,
> That awful Power rose from the mind's abyss
> Like an unfathered vapour that enwraps,

At once, some lonely traveller. I was lost;
Halted without an effort to break through;
But to my conscious soul I now can say—
'I recognise thy glory:' in such strength
Of usurpation, when the light of sense
Goes out, but with a flash that has revealed
The invisible world, doth greatness make abode,
There harbours; whether we be young or old,
Our destiny, our being's heart and home,
Is with infinitude, and only there;
With hope it is, hope that can never die,
Effort, and expectation, and desire,
And something evermore about to be.
Under such banners militant, the soul
Seeks for no trophies, struggles for no spoils
That may attest her prowess, blest in thoughts
That are their own perfection and reward,
Strong in herself and in beatitude
That hides her, like the mighty flood of Nile
Poured from his fount of Abyssinian clouds
To fertilise the whole Egyptian plain.   (VI, 592-616)

There is a close parallel between this experience of Words-worth's youth and his reaction to a scene during his tour of Italy in 1837. Disappointed at the view of the Capitolian Hill and the Tarpeian Rock, Wordsworth asks in the sonnet *At Rome*:

Is this, ye Gods, the Capitolian Hill?
Yon petty Steep in truth the fearful Rock,
Tarpeian named of yore, and keeping still
That name, a local Phantom proud to mock
The Traveller's expectation? — Could our Will
Destroy the ideal Power within, 'twere done
Thro' what men see and touch, — slaves wandering on,
Impelled by thirst of all but Heaven-taught skill.
Full oft, our wish obtained, deeply we sigh;
Yet not unrecompensed are they who learn,
From that depression raised, to mount on high

With stronger wing, more clearly to discern
Eternal things; and, if need be, defy
Change, with a brow not insolent, though stern.

Here is a more concise statement of the distinction between the immediate sense impressions which in themselves sometimes prove disappointing, and the power of the imagination to transform them into their proper position as parts of a meaningful whole.

There is little question but that the source of this sonnet is to be found in the following passage from Burnet's *Travels,* a book in Wordsworth's library at Rydal Mount:

It is certain, that when one is in the *Capitol,* and sees those poor Remains of what once it was, he is surprised to see a Building of so great a Fame sunk so low, that one can scarce imagine that it was once a Castle situated upon a Hill, able to hold out against a Siege of the *Gauls.* The *Tarpeian* Rock is now of so small a Fall, that a Man would think it no great Matter for his Diversion, to leap over it.[4]

If Wordsworth did base his sonnet on the passage in Burnet, his adaptation of that writer's description provides what we shall discover to be a not uncommon practice on his part of using concrete illustrations of ideas with which he was constantly grappling whenever he found them already verbalized in the writings of travelers and explorers who, in their time had looked steadily at their subject. Wordsworth's own comment on this sonnet in the Fenwick note suggests further the poet's debt to Burnet in starting the association of ideas that finally resulted in the poem. Characteristically, both in the prose commentary and in the sonnet itself, Wordsworth goes beyond his source in describing the power of the imagination to synthesize.

Sight is at first a sad enemy to imagination and to those pleasures belonging to old times with which some exertions of that power will always mingle: nothing perhaps brings this truth home to the feelings more than the city of Rome; not so much in respect to the impression made at the moment when it is first seen and looked at as a whole, for then the imagination may be invigorated and the mind's eye quickened. . . . But when particular spots or objects are sought out, disappointment is, I believe, invariably felt. Ability to recover from this disappointment will exist in proportion to knowledge, and the power of the mind to reconstruct out of fragments and parts, and to make details in the present subservient to more adequate comprehension of the past.

Another way in which Wordsworth attempted to suggest the limitation of our sense impression was to present "ordinary things . . . to the mind in an unusual aspect." His subject was not usually the mere fact or descriptive aspect of nature, not, for example, the mere description of daffodils, but the human emotions that the sight of daffodils suggested to the poet. Even so, Wordsworth depended on these sense impressions — the sights he saw, and the people he met on his walks — to provide him with the raw material on which his creative imagination could work. He frequently thought of his poetry as stemming chiefly from close personal observation combined with quiet contemplation. Of the first edition of *Lyrical Ballads* he remarks: "It may be proper to say that they are either absolute inventions of the author, or facts which took place within his personal observation or that of his friends." (In making this statement he obviously overlooked *The Complaint of a Forsaken Indian Woman,* whose source was Hearne's *Journey;* see *supra,* p. 14.)

Yet an analysis of several of his most characteristic poems reveals the fact that he often found verbal descriptions, such as recollections from his reading in travel books or the impressions of his trips recorded by Dorothy in her *Journal,* as useful as actual personal observation. For example, one of Wordsworth's most characteristic poems, and certainly one of his best known, is *I Wandered Lonely as a Cloud.* What poem could more adequately represent

Wordsworth's doctrine of choosing simple subjects and treating them in relatively plain language? Here certainly is "emotion recollected in tranquillity." And what poem could illustrate more clearly Wordsworth's habit of writing with his eye steadily on his subject? Here is a poem typical of one whose "study is out of doors," who composed, as he so frequently insists, while sitting by the side of a brook, standing in a grove, or walking along the road. Yet even in so obviously an out-of-doors poem, one that seems to be the result of first-hand observation, we find evidence that Wordsworth supplemented his own observations with descriptions that had already been verbalized. "The occasion which inspired the poem," de Selincourt tells us, "was on April 15, 1802, when W. and his sister 'were in the woods beyond Gowbarrow Park.' " He adds that the poem "is clearly indebted to D. W.'s *Journal* of that date:

'I never saw daffodils so beautiful. They grew among the mossy stones about and about them; some rested their heads upon these stones, as on a pillow, for weariness; and the rest tossed and reeled and danced, and seemed as if they verily laughed with the wind, that blew upon them over the lake; they looked so gay, ever glancing, ever changing.' " [5]

It would seem that part of this poem, especially the lines, "Fluttering and dancing in the breeze," and "Tossing their heads in sprightly dance," depends for its actual language, not only on what Wordsworth saw, but also on what Dorothy had already recorded in her *Journal*. We noted above that during the lapse of time between observation and composition, there often occurred a long period of contemplation on Wordsworth's part during which the multiplicity of his sense impressions was reduced to a meaningful image. If, as on this occasion, someone else has reduced the matter for him, or has shown him how to reduce it, he will make grateful use of the book. Here Wordsworth, in striving to select from the confused and complex imagery of his actual experience some-

thing that would have definite meaning, apparently fixed on Dorothy's image of social joy: "a long belt of [daffodils] along the
shore, about the breadth of a country turnpike road ... danced ...
laughed ... they looked so gay ... the simplicity, unity, and life
of that one busy highway." [6] Once this dominant image has been
seized upon, the poet will sometimes even change certain details
of his actual experience to achieve the emotional tone. Here, too,
a recorded account can be helpful. In this poem, in order to
heighten by contrast the idea of *social* derived from his sister's
Journal, he calls himself a "lonely" wanderer, which, in fact, he
was not. To convey the idea of *joy* more effectively, he reduces
Dorothy's accurate word *wind* ("It was a threatening, misty
morning. ... The wind was furious") to *breeze.* And he excluded
a number of very pretty images in Dorothy's account because they
would have detracted from the effect. For example, "some rested
their heads upon these stones as on a pillow for weariness." (The
idea of weariness is foreign to the effect he is trying to create.)
Thus the process of simplifying the complex and confusing mass of
actual experience is made easier when Wordsworth can work from
material where the process of selection has already been started by
others.[7]

In considering the genesis of this poem, one should not, however, overlook a passage in Bartram to which Lowes has called
attention:

Some of these roving beauties stroll over the mossy, shelving,
humid rocks, or from off the expansive wavy boughs of trees, bending
over the floods, salute their delusive shade, playing on the surface;
some plunge their perfumed heads and bathe their flexile limbs in
the silver stream; whilst others by the mountain breezes are tossed
about.[8]

Taken as a whole, the poem follows the passage from Dorothy's
Journal more closely than it does Bartram's sentence quoted above;

31

but the phrase in Bartram, "by the mountain breezes . . . tossed about," is as close to the wording of the poem as anything in the passage from the *Journal,* and may have suggested to Wordsworth the substitution of *breeze* for *wind.*

The Solitary Reaper is another poem in which Wordsworth apparently found descriptive phrases that had already been recorded as helpful as first-hand personal observation in composing a poem. During the tour of Scotland in 1803 he and his sister had seen "small companies of reapers" working in the fields. But the poem itself was suggested, not so much by this sight as "by a beautiful sentence in Thomas Wilkinson's *Tour in Scotland.*" [9] In a note to the edition of 1807, Wordsworth acknowledges his debt to Wilkinson, remarking: "This poem was suggested by a beautiful sentence in a MS Tour in Scotland written by a Friend, the last line being taken from it *verbatim.*" [10]

There is another possible source that has not been pointed out. It occurs in Robert Heron's *Observations of Scotland,* a book Wordsworth quotes from at length in a note to *The Excursion,* I, 341. The passage from Heron which, unconsciously or otherwise, may have suggested the phraseology of "The Solitary Reaper" is as follows:

As we entered the yard at the inn of Tayndrom, we heard the plaintive and simple notes of a Gaelic air sung to Gaelic words. . . . I was attracted by the music: For I have long since learned to admire the simple, native music of my country with all the fond enthusiasm of ignorance: And as I have not the happiness to understand Gaelic, it was natural for me to be pleased with the words of a Gaelic song. . . . It is a fact in the history of the manners of the Highlanders, that they are accustomed to sing at the performance of almost every piece of social labour: Rowers in a boat sing as they ply the oars; reapers sing as they cut down handful after handful of the corn; and here were washers singing as they rubbed and rinsed their clothes. This accompaniment of music certainly renders the labour more cheerful. [11]

Just how much this passage may have influenced Wordsworth cannot, of course, be positively determined. It is hard to believe that he did not derive at least the word *plaintive* from Heron's passage:

> Will no one tell me what she sings? —
> Perhaps the plaintive numbers flow
> For old, unhappy, far-off things,
> And battles long ago.

The debt may be greater, however; and Wordsworth who, like Heron, did not understand Gaelic, may have been reminded of the singing reapers he had encountered during his own tour of Scotland by reading Heron's remark that he was pleased with the words of the Gaelic song even though he did not understand them. Nor is the effectiveness of the poem impaired by its having been derived, in part at least, from second-hand sources rather than from personal observation. In the opinion of one critic, the clarity and simplicity of the poem owe much to the fact that Wordsworth wrote it, not so much out of his own recollection of what he had seen as from the accounts of other writers. Professor Havens writes, "The absence of needless detail in 'The Solitary Reaper' may be due to its having been suggested by something Wordsworth read, not by any specific incident in his recent Scottish tour." [12] This is perhaps just another way of saying that Wordsworth benefited from being able to work with material in which the elimination of irrelevant details, and the selection of those features that would give definite meaning to his poem, had already been started. In any case here is another poem that seems as though it should have sprung from Wordsworth's personal observation. Yet we find that, in its composition, Wordsworth's first-hand observation was supplemented by a sentence from Wilkinson and probably by a page from Heron's *Observations of Scotland*.

A passage in the poem, *To H. C. Six Years Old,* also demonstrates the fact that Wordsworth sometimes preferred to use material that had already been verbalized, even though he was working with a subject on which he could draw largely from his own personal observation. For example, Wordsworth, speaks of young Coleridge as

> Thou faery voyager! that dost float
> In such clear water, that thy boat
> May rather seem
> To brood on air than on an earthly stream;
> Suspended in a stream as clear as sky,
> Where earth and heaven do make one imagery.

In a note to the edition of 1807, Wordsworth acknowledges his debt to Carver with the following sentence: "See Carver's Description of his Situation upon one of the Lakes of America." The poet also refers to Carver and comments on the image described in the above-mentioned passage when he writes, in his *Guide to the Lakes*:

The water is also of crystalline purity; so that, if it were not for the reflections of the incumbent mountains by which it is darkened, a delusion might be felt, by a person resting quietly in a boat on the bosom of Winandermere or Derwent-water, similar to that which Carver so beautifully describes when he was floating alone in the middle of lake Erie or Ontario, and could almost have imagined that his boat was suspended in an element as pure as air, or rather that the air and water were one.[13]

Carver's description, from which Wordsworth borrows in the poem on Hartley Coleridge, is as follows:

The water in general appeared to lie on a bed of rocks. When it was calm, and the sun shone bright, I could sit in my canoe, where the depth was upwards of six fathoms, and plainly see huge piles of stone at the bottom, of different shapes, some of which appeared as if they were hewn. The water at this time was as pure and transparent as air; and my canoe seemed as if it hung suspended in that element."

The use he makes of this striking passage from Carver shows that the language and imagery of travel books often find their way into poems where Wordsworth could have relied on more direct and immediate sources. Obviously, the Lake Poet does not have to turn to books for information about the transparency of water, but he is struck by the felicitous expression in another writer of what he himself must have observed many times. Consequently, when he writes the poem to Hartley Coleridge he remembers Carver's unusual description as even more vivid than his own first-hand impressions.

Note also the different ways in which Wordsworth uses the description from Carver's *Travels*. In the *Guide*, he is writing literally and describing a phenomenon he has seen and that reminds him of the passage in Carver's account. In the poem, however, he makes figurative use of the description. When he writes of Hartley Coleridge as a faery voyager and pictures him in a boat, brooding on water so clear that it seems to be air, he is speaking metaphorically and trying to give an impression of the unearthliness of the child in somewhat the same way as he does in the *Intimations Ode* where he writes of the child coming from God and "trailing clouds of glory."

The Blind Highland Boy is another poem based on facts which took place within Wordsworth's personal observation or that of his friends. In the Fenwick note Wordsworth remarks: "The story was told me by George Mackereth, for many years parish-clerk of Grasmere. He had been an eye-witness of the occurrence." The poem is characteristic of Wordsworth's early experimental verse and has a definite kinship with poems like *The Idiot Boy, The Mad Mother, The Complaint of a Forsaken Indian Woman,* and *We are Seven.* It would appear to be simple, direct, and unrelated to literary sources. Yet the poem provides one of the most interesting illustrations of how Wordsworth changed a detail of the story by substituting for "reality" an incident furnished, this time by Coleridge's reading in a travel book.

The critic Jeffrey had objected violently to the following lines in *The Blind Highland Boy*:

> But say, what was it? Thought of fear!
> Well may ye tremble when ye hear!
> A household Tub, like one of those
> Which women use to wash their clothes,
> This carried the blind Boy.

"This," writes Jeffrey in the *Edinburgh Review* of October, 1807, "is carrying the matter as far as it will well go; nor is there anything,—down to the wiping of shoes, or the evisceration of chickens, —which may not be introduced in poetry, if this is tolerated."

In his notebooks for 1808-9 Coleridge, too, objects, though less violently, to the washing-tub and the awkward manner in which it is specified. He also adds the following suggestion, which Wordsworth incorporated into his revision of the poem for the edition of 1815:

Had I written the sweet tale of the 'Blind Highland Boy', I would have substituted for the washing-tub, and the awkward stanza in which it is specified, the images suggested in the following lines from Dampier's *Travels* Vol. I, pp. 105-6: — 'I heard of a monstrous green turtle once taken at the Port Royal, in the Bay of Campeachy, that was four feet deep from the back to the belly, and the belly six feet broad: Captain Rock's son of about nine or ten years of age, went in it as in a boat, on board his father's ship, about a quarter of a mile from the shore'. . . . Why might not some mariners [Coleridge adds] have left this shell on the shore of Loch Leven for awhile, about to have transported it inland for a curiosity, and the blind boy have found it? Would not the incident be in equal keeping with that of the child as well as the image and tone of romantic uncommonness? [15]

For good or ill (and there has been some disagreement among the critics), Wordsworth followed Coleridge's suggestion that he substitute a turtle shell for the wash tub. Besides this, he added several new verses to the poem in the edition of 1815 in which some of Dampier's material is used. Also, he has the boy hear of the turtle shell and of the adventure of Captain Rock's little son. This poem being "A Tale told by the Fire-side" presumably to a child, Wordsworth embellishes the factual language found in Dampier. Captain Rock's ship, which is not described by Dampier, becomes "that gallant ship of war"; Port Royal in the Bay of Campeachy becomes "the margin of a bay/Among the Indian isles." The following stanzas added in later versions are far more romantic than those of the original:

> But say what bears him? — Ye have seen
> The Indian's bow, his arrows keen,
> Rare beasts, and birds with plumage bright;
> Gifts which, for wonder or delight,
> Are brought in ships from far.
>
> Such gifts had those seafaring men
> Spread round that haven in the glen;
> Each hut, perchance, might have its own;
> And to the Boy they all were known —
> He knew and prized them all.
>
> The rarest was a Turtle-shell
> Which he, poor Child, had studied well;
> A shell of ample size, and light
> As the pearly car of Amphitrite,
> That sportive dolphins drew. . . .
>
> And this the little blind Boy knew;
> And he a story strange yet true
> Had heard, how in a shell like this
> An English Boy, O thought of bliss!

37

> Had stoutly launched from shore;
>
> Launched from the margin of a bay
> Among the Indian isles, where lay
> His father's ship, and had sailed far—
> To join that gallant ship of war,
> In his delightful shell.

None of these verses appeared in the edition of 1807, but their addition seems particularly appropriate to the tone of a romantic, fireside tale. The revised poem is characteristic both of Wordsworth's interest in the experiences of simple, rustic people and of the poet's habit of drawing upon material found in travel books to embellish his poetry. In this instance Wordsworth did well to modify the details of the story as he had originally heard it from George Mackereth; and the blending of the factual account drawn from Dampier with the "true story" that Wordsworth had heard from the parish clerk of Grasmere combined to make a poem much improved over the original.

Wordsworth used material from travel books, not only to help clarify and bring into focus the complex imagery of his own personal observations, but also to support certain tenets in his poetical credo. Sometimes he is struck by a passage because it seems to reenforce one of his beliefs; sometimes because the passage runs contrary to his theories of poetry. An example of the latter is found in *A Morning Exercise,* to which Wordsworth appends the following note: "See Waterton's Wanderings in South America." Professor Knight, in pointing out that "Muccawiss" (*Excursion,* III, 947) is an Indian word for whip-poor-will, calls attention to the use of the latter word in line 16 of *A Morning Exercise* and cites several passages in Waterton where the word *whip-poor-will* appears.[16] In one of these passages he has uncovered the source of *A Morning Exercise*:

When in thy hammock, should the thought of thy little crosses and disappointments, in thy ups and downs through life, break in upon thee, and throw thee into a pensive mood, the owl will bear thee company. She will tell thee that hard has been her fate too; and at intervals, "Whip-poor-Will" and "Willy come go," will take up the tale of sorrow. Ovid has told thee how the owl once boasted the human form, and lost it for a very small offence; and were the poet alive now, he would inform thee, that "Whip-poor-Will" and "Willy come go," are the shades of those poor African and Indian slaves, who died worn out and brokenhearted."

This passage might be overlooked because of Knight's preoccupation with the word *Muccawiss;* in any case, he does not comment on the similarities and differences between this passage and the following two stanzas from *A Morning Exercise*:

> FANCY, who leads the pastimes of the glad,
> Full oft is pleased a wayward dart to throw;
> Sending sad shadows after things not sad,
> Peopling the harmless fields with signs of woe:
> Beneath her sway, a simple forest cry
> Becomes an echo of man's misery.
>
> Blithe ravens croak of death; and when the owl
> Tries his two voices for a favourite strain —
> *Tu-whit — Tu-whoo!* the unsuspecting fowl
> Forebodes mishap or seems but to complain;
> Fancy, intent to harass and annoy,
> Can thus pervert the evidence of joy.

Although the similarity between these two passages is obvious, the difference is significant also. Waterton remarks that when man is "pensive" and disappointed, the birds' songs will express sympathy with him, will "take up his tale of sorrow"; whereas Wordsworth shows that, though Fancy has the power to interpret a "simple forest cry" so that it becomes "an echo of man's misery," the birds' songs are *essentially* happy ones. Wordsworth's insistence that Fancy is perverting the "evidence of joy" by "sending sad shadows after things not sad" suggests the poet's disapproval of indulging in melancholy.

Another passage in Waterton that Wordsworth must have recalled for *A Morning Exercise* is the following:

> Four other species of the Goatsucker articulate some words so distinctly, that they have received their names from the sentences they utter, and absolutely bewilder the stranger on his arrival in these parts. . . . Another bids you, "Work-away, work-work-work-away." A third cries, mournfully, "Willy-come-go. Willy-Willy-Willy-come-go." And high up in the country, a fourth tells you to "Whip-poor-Will. Whip-whip-whip-poor-Will."

> You will never persuade the negro to destroy these birds, or get the Indian to let fly his arrow at them. They are birds of omen, and reverential dread. . . . They are the receptacles for departed souls, who come back again to earth . . . to haunt cruel and hard-hearted masters, and retaliate injuries received from them.[18]

The second paragraph in this passage from Waterton sheds some light on the rather puzzling third stanza of Wordsworth's poem:

> Through border wilds where naked Indians stray,
> Myriads of notes attest her subtle skill;
> A feathered task-master cries, "WORK AWAY!"
> And in thy iteration, "WHIP POOR WILL!"
> Is heard the spirit of a toil-worn slave,
> Lashed out of life, not quiet in the grave.

Earlier in this chapter we touched upon Wordsworth's break with his contemporaries both in subject matter and in phraseology. The poem under discussion bears out, both Professor Havens' statement that Wordsworth had none of the "sentimentalism of the eighteenth century graveyard poets" or the morbidness of the later romantics,[19] and Wordsworth's own conviction that poets are "the happiest of all men." [20]

On considering the subject matter of the poems just discussed, it becomes clear that Wordsworth's theory of poetry, as he himself put it into practice, was to widen considerably the range of material henceforth to be accepted as literature. In spite of protests by critics like Jeffrey against the inclusion, under the name of literature, of poems describing small boys in wash tubs, the tendency since Wordsworth's day has been to include, even to stress, homely details that an earlier age would have excluded as commonplace and low.

An examination of Wordsworth's diction has been omitted because, in spite of the poet's insistence that he was going to employ a "language really used by men," it remained for later writers, men like Whitman and Steinbeck, for instance, to parallel Wordsworth's leveling process in subject matter with a comparable realism in diction. That Wordsworth did not accomplish in any large measure, though it should be observed that he did use somewhat more realistic language than that employed by his younger contemporaries, Shelley and Keats, whose preference for allegorical language and figures involving myths, did not always please the Lake Poet. Perhaps Wordsworth's rather mild praise of Keats' "Hymn to Pan" from *Endymion,* which the older poet characterized as "a very pretty piece of paganism!" [21] on hearing it read, can be accounted for by Wordsworth's insistence that he wished to keep his readers "in the company of flesh and blood." However moderate Wordsworth's innovations in language may have been, in his characterization of ordinary men, including the rustic, the savage, and the simple child, he sought to extol those broad democratic and equalitarian principles characteristic of the nineteenth century. Therefore, it was to be expected that he would base his writings solidly upon a careful observation of men and manners. It follows, also, that his first-hand observation might effectively be supplemented and reenforced by his reading in the works of explorers and travellers.

CHAPTER TWO

TRAVEL BOOKS AND WORDSWORTH'S INTEREST IN PRIMITIVISM

WORDSWORTH'S INTEREST IN CHILDREN AND IN RUSTIC AND PRIMI-tive people, his love of simplicity and solitude, his concern with local customs and traditions, his enthusiasm for the patriot fighting against tyranny — all these typically romantic ideas and interests which recur again and again in his poetry — are to be found in the travel books he read. To a larger extent than has been realized, these books provided a significant source of his ideas, and it is the purpose of this chapter to show how important an influence his reading in travel books exerted in supplying ideas for his poetry. That this reading is related to basic concepts in Wordsworth's thinking has already been suggested by Professor Havens in the following passage from *The Mind of a Poet*:

> His love of wandering . . . and of romance . . . as well as his emphasis of fear . . . and wonder . . . show that this fondness for the literature of travel was connected with things that lay deep with him.[1]

Before beginning our discussion of Wordsworth's interest in rustic and primitive people, it may be well to set up some definitions. Lovejoy and Boas define primitivism as an attempt to answer the question "as to the time — past or present or future — at which the most excellent condition of human life, or the best state of the world in general, must be supposed to occur." Although not necessarily opposed to the idea of progress, primitivism tends to look backward in searching for evidence of an ideal state, since it grows out of the

discontent of the civilized with civilization, or with some conspicuous

43

and characteristic feature of it. It is the belief of men living in a relatively highly evolved and complex cultural condition that a life far simpler and less sophisticated in some or in all respects is a more desirable life. . . . The cultural primitivist has almost invariably believed that the simpler life of which he has dreamed has been somewhere, at some time, actually lived by human beings. He has not merely enunciated an ideal but has pointed to its exemplars.

To show the relation between primitivism and romanticism, Lovejoy and Boas continue:

The cultural primitivist's model of human excellence and happiness is sought . . . in the mode of life of existing primitive, or so-called 'savage' peoples . . . one of the roots of primitivism [is] the charm of the remote and strange, the craving to imagine, and even to experience, some fashion of life which is at least *different* . . . the love of strangeness and the revolt against the familiar is an element in cultural primitivism.[2]

In *Rousseau and Romanticism* Professor Babbitt lists the following characteristics of primitivism: the primitivist looks back to the dawn of history for his standard of excellence; he seeks to be like the new-born child; he praises spontaneity rather than imitation, nature rather than artifice; he champions the weak against the oppression of tyrannical government; he regards science and the arts as contrary to nature.[3]

It is unnecessary to dwell at length on the connection between the doctrine of primitivism and the romantic movement or, more particularly, Wordsworth's romantic interests. A list of several ideas common to both will show how close this relationship is: faith in the perfectibility of man, interest in the remote and the strange, a distrust of the complexity of civilized life, interest in the child and the common man, in the weak and the lowly as opposed to the strong. In illustrating Wordsworth's interest in primitivism we shall include, not only the noble savage, but also the rustic dalesman and the Swiss mountaineer. According to Professor Fairchild, Wordsworth would have been shocked at the thought of comparing the peasants of the Lake Country and of Switzerland with savages. "Nevertheless," Fairchild adds, "the comparison is tempting. One may at least say that the dalesman and the Noble Savage are similarly motivated. They spring from the same revulsion against corrupt civilization, and preach fundamentally the same gospel of innocent simplicity." [4] Further on he adds that the savage may also be grouped with the child and with the poet of nature in that all three rely more upon intuition than upon reason. Therefore, in treating Wordsworth's interest in primitivism, we shall draw on examples of primitive attributes, even though these are sometimes found in other than savage peoples.

Wordsworth's interest in primitivism stems in part from his independent boyhood spent in the country among rustic shepherds and mountaineers. Most biographers stress the influence of his free and easy childhood at Cockermouth and his school days at Hawkshead as contributing to his love of simplicity and his faith in nature so characteristic of the primitive. In the opening chapters of *The Lost Leader,* for example, Hugh Fausset points out that, because Wordsworth's first years were not marred by unnecessary parental regulation, "William was never in danger of being civilised before his time. He preserved intact those 'motions of savage instinct' which are native to the child, and may prove in time the rich soil of a vital imagination." [5] After his mother's death when he was not quite eight, Wordsworth was sent to school at Hawkshead. Here Wordsworth's liberty was not seriously impaired; for, since school began about six in the morning, the boys were allowed two hours of freedom at noon and were also at liberty from about four in the afternoon until evening. Fausset also mentions an attribute of the primitive which, like the other characteristics, Wordsworth was to experience in his everyday life before he began to think about it reflectively. This was the primitive or savage belief that the forces of nature possess the power of intervening purposively in human affairs. Fausset cites as an example the incident of the borrowed skiff and the passage from *The Prelude* (I, 357-400), in which Wordsworth recounts how the "huge peak . . . Upreared its head [and] Strode after me," as if it were Nature herself threatening to reprove and punish. It was very seldom, however, as Fausset goes on to tell, "that the primeval overpowered him to this degree." "His more familiar experience of Nature [was] as a 'beloved Presence.' " [6]

Since the effect of Wordsworth's tour of the Alps in 1790 will be discussed in connection with his reading in Coxe and Ramond, we shall here skip over the Cambridge period (October, 1787 — January, 1791) and consider Wordsworth's early attitude toward the French Revolution, especially as it was shaped by his friend, Michel Beaupuy. Fausset thus describes the French soldier with whom Wordsworth spent several months during his visit to France in 1791-2:

> To the humblest he was courteous without a hint of condescension and with a kind of radiant joy in the felt fact of his common humanity. And because his belief in the principle of human equality . . . grew out of a loving respect for the rights of every personality . . . he valued equally all that made men unique and all that bound them together. . . . Such a man was ideally and fatally formed to confirm Wordsworth's belief in the Revolutionary Movement. . . . In Beaupuy he saw the justification of every dream of human perfectibility. And . . . he regarded him as the pattern of the emancipated man whom Nature intended and whom the Revolution, by co-operating with Nature, would bring to birth. [7]

It may have been through Beaupuy, according to Professor Beatty, that Wordsworth first became familiar with Ramond's translation of Coxe's *Travels in Switzerland*.[8] In those travelers' accounts of the heroic and democratic qualities of Swiss mountaineers, Wordsworth was to find his own theories regarding the potential greatness of the common man substantiated.

There is, however, some evidence in Wordsworth's letter to his sister, written while he was still on the tour (September 6, 1790), to suggest that he had read Coxe or Ramond *before* setting forth. While outlining the itinerary of his journey, Wordsworth explains to Dorothy: "You have undoubtedly heard of these celebrated scenes, but if you have not read of them, any description which I have here room to give you must be altogether inadequate." Does this not suggest that Wordsworth had already read some descriptions of these "celebrated scenes" and was in a position to compare his own account of them in the letter with the more detailed accounts to be found in a book like Coxe's? Many of the points of interest referred to by the poet in his letter, including Lucerne, Einsiedlen, Glarus, Como, the country of the Grisons, and Altdorf, are described in detail by Coxe. Further on in the letter there is another remark which strongly suggests that he had read Coxe's *Travels*. Writing about the Rhine at Schaffhausen, Wordsworth says: "Magnificent as this fall certainly is, I must confess I was disappointed in it. I had raised my ideas too high." [9] One might ask when and where he had raised his ideas too high. Was it while reading a description of this fall in Coxe? If he had read Coxe at all before starting on his tour, he would have come across the description of the fall which occurs in the second chapter. And Coxe's description would have raised Wordsworth's expectation to the highest pitch:

Advancing to the edge of the precipice which overhangs the Rhine, we looked down perpendicularly upon the cataract, and saw the river tumbling over the sides of the rock with amazing violence and precipitation . . . the sea of foam rushing down — the continual cloud of spray scattered to a great distance, and to a considerable height — in short, the magnificence of the whole scenery far surpassed my most sanguine expectations, and exceeds all description.[10]

From the remarks contained in Wordsworth's letter, it is evident that he must have read some account of Switzerland before setting off on his tour; it is not unlikely that the book he read was Coxe's *Travels,* a volume which by 1790 had been ten years before the public. The enthusiasm for the Alps communicated by his reading of this book would provide a plausible explanation of his erratic behavior in leaving Cambridge just when he should have been studying for his examinations.

Whether Wordsworth read Coxe and Ramond before or after the tour of 1790, both the tour and the reading aroused his interest in the ideal setting of primeval man and the perfect democratic community. From his earliest years itinerant peddlars, mountaineers, and Indians all appealed to him as appropriate subjects for poetic treatment. And although he learned much about some of these types through first-hand observation, we find that in many of his poems he apparently preferred to draw upon characters and traits of character that had already been described by the explorers and adventurers whose travel books he was so fond of reading. How he modified these characters to suit his poetic purposes will be especially important to observe. Frequently he portrayed primitive or rustic people in the grip of an emotional crisis; Ina in *The Russian Fugitive* and the dying mother in *The Complaint of a Forsaken Indian Woman* are two examples. Sometimes he was attracted to rustic characters because they served to illustrate some major tenet of his faith, such as the belief that man has a better chance to develop morally and spiritually when he lives in a little village or in the mountains.

Before analyzing several poems in which Wordsworth borrows various details about primitive and rustic people from his reading in travel books, we should attempt to explain the particular nature of his primitivism. First of all, in spite of his enthusiasm for the idyllic description of savage life found in the writings of Bartram and others, one never thinks of Wordsworth as ready to pull up stakes and settle in a wild, uncivilized region. Travel and wandering he enjoyed thoroughly; but, unlike Coleridge and Southey, he never seriously considered "trying the experiment of perfectibility on the banks of the Susquehanna." [11] The plain living and high thinking at which he aimed in his own life he meant to achieve within the existing frame of English society; he wanted to live in the country rather than in the city, but not necessarily in the unspoiled wilderness. And in spite of his rhapsodic utterance in *The Prelude* (III, 430 ff.), in which he longs for "a sanctuary for our country's youth . . . [in] a primeval grove," it is not necessary to conclude that in fact he ever advocated transplanting Cambridge University to America. Unlike Thoreau who chose (for a time) to turn his back upon existing society and went to the woods because he "wished to live deliberately, to front only the essential facts of life," [12] Wordsworth preferred to live in society and to bring to the attention of his readers the simplicity of primitive life in the hope that they might learn from these rustics something that could be incorporated into the pattern of their lives to give them meaning and to rid them of the welter of details that confuses and depresses civilized man. What he liked about primitivism was that it appeared to be a simplifying movement, and both in his theory of poetry and in his personal life he aimed at simplification, attempting to lessen the confusion and extravagance of civilized life.

At first glance the term primitive seems not to apply to Wordsworth's politics, especially if we think of his mature convictions and the praise of Burke introduced into *The Prelude* some time after 1820. The story of his youthful revolutionary enthusiasm with its sequel of a somewhat stolid conservatism in later life is familiar enough, though probably it has become oversimplified in the minds of most of us. Wordsworth himself insisted that his fundamental belief in freedom never changed, although changing circumstances in the affairs of nations made him favor revolutionary France at one period and oppose her later. In a letter to James Losh (December 4, 1821) he answered the charge of apostasy as follows:

I should think that I had lived to little purpose if my notions on the subject of Government had undergone no modification. . . . If I were addressing those who have dealt so liberally with the words Renegado, Apostate, etc., I should retort the charge upon them, and say, *you* have been deluded by *Places* and *Persons,* while I have stuck to *Principles—I* abandoned France, and her Rulers, when *they* abandoned the struggle for Liberty, gave themselves up to Tyranny, and endeavoured to enslave the world.[13]

On the basis of his love of freedom he also looked back with disfavor on England's war against the American colonies and her interference with France in the early stages of the Revolution, since he felt that no nation, least of all England, the mother of freedom, should thwart the will of the people to choose their own form of government. But a glance at a passage from his *Apology for the French Revolution* reveals that, even in 1793, when Wordsworth was at an age with which one associates excessive optimism and enthusiasm, he was not blinded by faith in the natural goodness of man.

Appearing, as I do, the advocate of Republicanism, let me not be misunderstood. I am well aware, from the abuse of the executive power in States, that there is not a single European nation but what affords a melancholy proof that if, at this moment, the original authority of the people should be restored, all that could be expected from such restoration would in the beginning be but a change of tyranny.[14]

And a year later, in a letter to Mathews, Wordsworth expresses a horror of revolutionary violence. "The destruction of those Institutions which I condemn appears to me to be hastening on too rapidly. I recoil from the bare idea of a Revolution." [15] In the first of these passages, with its reference to the "original authority of the people," we are reminded of Wordsworth's primitivistic statement in *Descriptive Sketches*:

> Once Man entirely free, alone and wild,
> Was bless'd as free—for he was Nature's child. (520-1)

But in what follows we see that Wordsworth's faith and hope were not boundless; and that he recognized, even as a young man, the difficulties of restoring "natural" rights to man, and the dangers of violence. This evidence of conservatism or caution in his youth can be balanced by several liberal statements from his maturer years, as Edith Batho points out in her chapter on Wordsworth's politics.[16] For example, his attitude toward Italy, expressed in some of the *Memorials of a Tour in Italy, 1837,* and in the Fenwick notes, shows that his feelings for oppressed nations did not die out with advanced age.

But more important than trying to show that Wordsworth may have been more conservative in his youth and more liberal in later life than is generally supposed, is the evidence to be derived from his poetry, evidence that, whatever his stand on particular political issues, his general theory embraced an *abiding* faith in the common man. Let us consider several poems in which he has taken illustrations of rustic or primitive characteristics from his reading in travel books. Not all of these poems, it must be admitted, reveal the primitive in a favorable light. The young man in *Ruth* and the "squalid creature" in *The Excursion* represent, partly for dramatic purposes, the unfavorable aspects of primitivism. Nor do all the poems reveal Wordsworth's mature views. The first one to be examined, *Descriptive Sketches,* was written under the influence of Wordsworth's youthful enthusiasm for the French Revolution. Considered as a group, however, these poems stand as compelling evidence, both of the poet's interest in the primitive and the extent of his debt to travel books in supplying characters and incidents.

To begin with, it can be shown that the admiration revealed in *Descriptive Sketches* for the democratic Swiss cantons and for the free and simple life of the Swiss mountaineer — a feeling derived in part from his tour, in part from his reading in Coxe and Ramond — constitutes a permanent and significant aspect of his thinking. In the preparation of this poem Wordsworth leaned heavily on Ramond's translation of Coxe's *Travels in Switzerland*. He referred specifically to his borrowings from Ramond in three notes to the poem, and Legouis and Beatty have pointed out numerous other borrowings or similarities, amounting to about thirty in all.[17] It is certain, therefore, that Wordsworth was well acquainted with this book before 1793. In examining Wordsworth's borrowings from Ramond one finds that they set a pattern to be followed in his later poetry when he had occasion to refer to other books of travel. In the *Descriptive Sketches* and, to a lesser extent, in that portion of *The Prelude* concerned with his walking tour (VI, 322-778), Wordsworth reveals a consuming interest in rustic and primitive men. Since his representation of the Swiss mountaineer as approximating the "ideal" man is of paramount importance, let us consider that first.

In *Descriptive Sketches* Wordsworth represents the Swiss mountaineer as bearing the traces of primeval man, free and restrained by none, obeying no law except that dictated by his reason:

> Once Man entirely free, alone and wild,
> Was bless'd as free — for he was Nature's child.
> He, all superior but his God disdain'd,
> Walk'd none restraining, and by none restrain'd,
> Confess'd no law but what his reason taught,
> Did all he wish'd, and wish'd but what he ought.
> As Man in his primaeval dower array'd
> The image of his glorious sire display'd
> Ev'n so, by vestal Nature guarded, here
> The traces of primaeval Man appear.
> The native dignity no forms debase,
> The eye sublime, and surly lion-grace.
> The slave of none, of beasts alone the lord,
> He marches with his flute, his book, and sword,

> Well taught by that to feel his rights, prepar'd
> With this "the blessings he enjoys to guard."   (520-35)

A similar idea is advanced by Coxe and Ramond in the sixth letter on the Canton of Glarus. The former first relates the glorious victories of the Swiss over their Austrian oppressors in the fourteenth century:

> These surprising victories, gained by a handful of men against an enemy so much superior in number . . . render the wonderful combats of Marathon and Plataea . . . perfectly credible. The same love of independence, the same dread of slavery, and the same attachment to their country, animated the respective nations to the same deeds of heroism; and in both instances victory was followed by the same glorious consequences: for the Swiss, as well as the Greeks, owe the rise and preservation of their liberties to that magnanimous and determined valour, which prefers death to living under the servile domination of an arbitrary despot.[18]

Then, after describing the scenery, commenting on the commerce and exports, and on the simplicity of their homes and the excellence of their food, Coxe concludes as follows:

> Nothing delights me so much as the inside of a Swiss cottage: all those I have hitherto visited, convey the liveliest image of cleanliness, ease and simplicity; and cannot but strongly impress upon the observer a most pleasing conviction of the peasant's happiness.
>
> If I had never seen these little democratical states, I could have formed no idea of the general equality and indistinction that prevails among the inhabitants. . . . If that sort of government be confessedly the best, which constitutes the greatest good of the greatest number in the community; these little states . . . may justly claim a large share of our approbation. General liberty, general independence, and an exemption from arbitrary taxes, are blessings which amply compensate for a want of those refinements that are introduced by opulence and luxury.[19]

Ramond's added comment, in his chapter on the same canton, emphasizes the part that the protective natural setting of Glarus played in marking it as a stronghold of freedom:

Quand on ne sauroit pas que ces énormes amas sont le grand attelier de la nature & le réservoir de nos fleuves, on ne s'étonneroit point qu'elle eût fait la dépense de ce mur inébranlable, pour enclore une terre qu'elle semble avoir destinée à être l'inviolable asyle de la liberté. [Ramond's footnote follows:] (2) La Suisse a été marquée par la nature pour être libre; les considérations de la politique & les fantaisies des Conquérans ne peuvent rien contre la volonté de la nature. Dans les tems mêmes où la Suisse connoissoit des maîtres, elle avoit des *priviléges,* des *exemptions,* des *libertés,* elle étoit Républicaine, & l'oppression n'a jamais pesé sur elle qu'autant qu'il falloit pour lui apprendre qu'elle étoit faite pour être libre.[20]

It should be noted that, in the opening lines of *Descriptive Sketches,* Wordsworth has followed Ramond in asserting that "the mountain-side," the "Unfathom'd dells and undiscover'd woods," provide the ideal habitation for free men. And some ten or twelve years later, in *The Prelude,* he writes of the Swiss Cantons as "Those sanctified abodes of peaceful man" (VI, 508). Observe the number of ideas admired by the primitivists that appear in *Descriptive Sketches* and stem from Wordsworth's reading in Coxe and Ramond: man living free and unrestrained, resisting tyranny and oppression, and experiencing the simple joys of a child of nature in a charming natural environment. Compare this with Lovejoy and Boas' description of the individual in primitive society who has "been pictured as relatively exempt from constraint by the social group, more free to do as he pleases; his native impulses and emotions and modes of self-expression . . . not yet . . . confined in a strait-jacket."[21]

But while civilized man admires the primitive because his life seems simpler, because he is satisfied with less and is consequently free from the hard labor which civilization demands, at the same time primitive man is admired because his life is, in some respects, harder and fraught with greater danger. Wordsworth, who admires the Swiss because of their simplicity and independence, also writes of the dangers encountered by the Swiss mountaineers:

> Ye dewy mists the arid rocks o'er-spread
> Whose slippery face derides his deathful tread!
> —To wet the peak's impracticable sides
> He opens of his feet the sanguine tides,
> Weak and more weak the issuing current eyes
> Lapp'd by the panting tongue of thirsty skies.
> —At once bewildering mists around him close,
> And cold and hunger are his least of woes;
> The Demon of the snow with angry roar
> Descending, shuts for aye his prison door.   (392-401)

Here his source is a passage in Ramond (I, 271-5) which Beatty summarizes as "an elaborate account of these interesting people, representing the simplest form of society and possessing the ultimate virtues of independence and liberty; suffering incredible hardships, and venturing upon rocks where they must open their veins to obtain a precarious foothold." [22]

It is apparent, then, that the reading of Coxe and Ramond had a share in formulating and crystalizing Wordsworth's theories regarding the worth and dignity of primitive men, an idea that was soon to find expression in the "Preface to the *Lyrical Ballads*" where Wordsworth tells us that, for the subject matter of his poetry he chose humble and rustic life. It is doubtful whether Wordsworth's first-hand acquaintance with the Swiss made during the tour of 1790 would have accounted, by itself, for the early development of this idea; it is equally doubtful whether the reading of travel books without the exhilaration provided by the tour could have stimulated Wordsworth to poetic achievement. But, on this early occasion, as in later life, travel and the reading of travel books combined to provide the proper inspiration for his poetry. As Professor Lowes remarks in his detailed study of Coleridge's sources, this is one of those occasions where "things read have blended with things seen." [23]

Among the books of travel mentioned by Wordsworth in various notes to the *Lyrical Ballads* are the *Travels of William Bartram* and Samuel Hearne's *Journey from Hudson's Bay to the Northern Ocean.* The use to which he puts some of his borrowings from these travel books shows that his concern with rustic and primitive types, already evident in the *Descriptive Sketches,* is still present. But in those selections from the *Lyrical Ballads* we are about to discuss, his purpose is not to exalt the virtues of mountaineers; instead, he is concerned with analyzing human emotions, particularly the emotions of primitive people, or children, in times of stress. At the same time, as we shall see in considering such poems as *The Complaint of a Forsaken Indian Woman* and *The Idiot Boy,* Wordsworth's belief in the innate goodness of simple people living in natural rather than artificial surroundings, is apparent in much of his characterization.

A typical example of this interest and of Wordsworth's technique is to be found in *The Complaint of a Forsaken Indian Woman.* In his preface to that poem, he acknowledges in some detail his indebtedness to Samuel Hearne's *Journey*:

> When a Northern Indian, from sickness, is unable to continue his journey with his companions, he is left behind, covered over with deer-skins, and is supplied with water, food, and fuel, if the situation of the place will afford it. He is informed of the track which his companions intend to pursue, and if he be unable to follow, or overtake them, he perishes alone in the desert, unless he should have the good fortune to fall in with some other tribes of Indians. The females are equally, or still more, exposed to the same fate. See that very interesting work Hearne's "Journey from Hudson's Bay to the Northern Ocean".

How closely Wordsworth follows Hearne, both in phraseology and incident, and in what respects he differs from his source, may be seen by examining Hearne's account in the seventh chapter of his *Journey*:

> One of the Indian's wives, who for some time had been in a consumption, had for a few days past become so weak as to be incapable of travelling, which, among those people, is the most deplorable state to which a human being can possibly be brought. Whether she had been given over by the doctors, or that it was for want of friends among them, I cannot tell, but certain it is, that no expedients were taken for her recovery; so that, without much ceremony, she was left unassisted, to perish above-ground. . . .
>
> On those occasions, therefore, the friends or relations of the sick generally leave them some victuals and water; and, if the situation of the place will afford it, a little firing. When those articles are provided, the person to be left is acquainted with the road which the others intend to go; and then, after covering them well up with deer skins, &c. they take their leave, and walk away crying.
>
> Sometimes persons thus left, recover; and come up with their friends, or wander about till they meet with other Indians, whom they accompany till they again join their relations. Instances of this kind are seldom known. The poor woman above mentioned, however, came up with us three several times, after having been left in the manner described. At length, poor creature! she dropt behind, and no one attempted to go back in search of her.[24]

In his poem Wordsworth uses several of the details found in Hearne. He refers to the fire, food, and water left, as was the custom, for the forsaken woman. But whereas Hearne merely states baldly that "sometimes persons . . . recover and come up with their friends," Wordsworth lets us see the despair in the deserted woman's mind:

> Alas! ye might have dragged me on
> Another day, a single one!
> Too soon I yielded to despair;
> Why did ye listen to my prayer?
> When ye were gone my limbs were stronger;
> And oh, how grievously I rue,

> That, afterwards, a little longer,
> My friends, I did not follow you!
> For strong and without pain I lay,
> Dear friends, when ye were gone away.

In the explorer's factual account, emphasis is placed upon this curious and, to our way of thinking, heartless custom. But Wordsworth changes this emphasis upon incident, and focuses our attention upon character; he makes his poem a dramatic monologue in which he reveals the feeling of a young mother facing death alone. To accentuate this emotional aspect of the poem, Wordsworth introduces a detail not found in Hearne. He has the woman separated from her infant child:

> My child! they gave thee to another,
> A woman who was not thy mother.
> When from my arms my Babe they took,
> On me how strangely did he look!
> Through his whole body something ran,
> A most strange working did I see;
> —As if he strove to be a man,
> That he might pull the sledge for me:
> And then he stretched his arms, how wild!
> Oh mercy! like a helpless child.

She is also represented as a child of nature living in harmony with her surroundings and in sympathy with every living thing. Note the following four lines from an "overflow" cited by de Selincourt:

> Why do I watch those running deer,
> And wherefore wherefore come they here?
> And wherefore do I seem to love
> The things that live, the things that move? [25]

This emphasis on the forsaken woman's feelings is not found in Hearne; for, even though Wordsworth's poems often contain material found in travel books, his purpose in borrowing from them was not merely to reproduce in poetical language certain curious and out-of-the-way facts. Instead, he found in those books the raw material out of which to construct poems that would portray the emotions of real people in representative situations of life. As he tells us in the "Preface to the *Lyrical Ballads*," his purpose was "to follow the fluxes and refluxes of the mind when agitated by the great and simple affections of our nature . . . by accompanying the last struggles of a human being at the approach of death, cleaving in solitude to life and society, as in the Poem of the FORSAKEN INDIAN." Sometimes he could find these representative situations in his own experiences, in his travels, in his talks with pedlars and other rustic characters; on other occasions, such as this one, he relied on the realistic accounts of explorers and travelers.

When one compares the poem just discussed with its source, and notes the shift in emphasis from the narrating by Hearne of a harsh and Spartan-like Indian custom to the characterization by Wordsworth of tender, motherly feelings in the forsaken Indian, one might conclude that Wordsworth was not looking steadily at his subject and was glossing over facts. However, as we shall see in discussing *Ruth* and the "squalid creature" in *The Excursion,* Wordsworth was quite capable of depicting the wicked or ugly side of his children of nature when that type of characterization suited his purpose.

Discussion of the forsaken Indian woman brings to mind another character that Wordsworth discovered while reading travel books. Although Ina, in *The Russian Fugitive,* is not actually a primitive, she embodies those primitive virtues which Wordsworth liked to contrast with the vices of civilization. Consequently, an analysis of *The Russian Fugitive* seems appropriate here because this poem provides an excellent example of the extent to which whole episodes from a travel book sometimes find their way into Wordsworth's poems and are adapted to his purposes.

In a note to the poem Wordsworth writes: "Peter Henry Bruce, having given in his entertaining Memoirs the substance of his Tale, affirms that, besides the concurring reports of others, he had the story from the lady's own mouth." The passage to which Wordsworth alludes appears in Book III of Bruce's *Memoirs*.

Wordsworth follows the traveler's account closely, omitting some details and elaborating on others so that his poem has the tone of a medieval narrative of injured innocence. For example, in the story as related by Bruce, the Czar meets a young woman while dining at the house of her father, a foreign merchant: "He was so much taken with her appearance, that he offered her any terms she pleased, if she would live with him; which this virtuous young woman modestly refused, but dreading the effects of his authority, she . . . left Moscow in the night, without communicating her design even to her parents." [26] Wordsworth's poem begins with a young woman, whom he names Ina, bribing a guard to open the gates of Moscow so that she may escape:

> Through Moscow's gates, with gold unbarred,
> Stepped One at dead of night,
> Whom such high beauty could not guard
> From meditated blight;
> By stealth she passed, and fled as fast
> As doth the hunted fawn,
> Nor stopped, till in the dappling east
> Appeared unwelcome dawn.   (I, 9-16)

She continues her flight and for "Seven nights her course renewed," hiding in the fields by day. (In Bruce's version, she merely "travelled on foot several miles into the country, till she arrived at a small village where her nurse lived.")

In the poem, once her escape has been effected, Ina is concerned, not only for her own safety, but for that of her foster-parents to whom she has fled. Though they insist that "For you we both would die," she prefers to hide on an island in the middle of

> a treacherous swamp,
> On which the noonday sun shed light
> As from a lonely lamp.   (II, 98-100)

This "sanctuary . . . From all intrusion free" is Wordsworth's romantic counterpart of Bruce's "little dry spot in the middle of a morass [where the nurse's husband, in the prose account] built a hut for her habitation." According to Bruce, "She had deposited her money with her nurse to procure little necessaries for her support, which were faithfully conveyed to her at night by the nurse or her daughter, by one of whom she was constantly attended in the night-time." These regular nightly visits Wordsworth changes into rare occasions of delight for the lonely young girl dwelling "in solitude," taming the birds and cultivating the flowers, and thinking of her parents and her home in France.

> And oft, as either Guardian came,
> The joy in that retreat
> Might any common friendship shame,
> So high their hearts would beat;
> And to the lone Recluse, whate'er
> They brought, each visiting
> Was like the crowding of the year
> With a new burst of spring.   (III, 217-24)

Ina's self-imposed exile is to last only a year, however, before she is discovered, in Bruce's account by "a colonel who had come from the army to see his friends, going a hunting into that wood, and following his game through the morass . . . came to the hut, and looking into it saw a pretty young woman in a mean dress." In the poem, Bruce's colonel becomes a hunter endowed with the chivalry of a medieval knight-errant; (Wordsworth calls him a

"Cavalier.") When he pursues a wounded deer to the very door of Ina's bower, she decides to throw herself upon his mercy:

> "In me
> Behold," she said, "a stricken Hind
> Pursued by destiny!
>
> "From your deportment, Sir! I deem
> That you have worn a sword,
> And will not hold in light esteem
> A suffering woman's word."   (IV, 278-84)

In relating her hardships, she complains not of "the winter's cold" nor "summer's heat" nor yet of her estrangement from "social life." Rather, she affirms that

> "High Heaven is my defence;
> And every season has soft arms
> For injured Innocence.
>
> "From Moscow to the Wilderness
> It was my choice to come,
> Lest virtue should be harbourless,
> And honour want a home."   (IV, 302-8)

The hunter at once recognizes her as the lady "Whose vanishing was rumoured wide,/Sad theme for every tongue." He immediately falls in love with her and decides to ask Lady Catherine of Russia to intervene in her behalf. After he has been assured that the Emperor will grant a full pardon, Ina returns to marry the hunter, while "universal Moscow shared/The triumph of that hour."

Bruce's version differs here in several respects: in his account there is no mention of love at first sight; the colonel goes first to the girl's parents, and they together consult Catherine as to how best to broach to the Emperor the subject of the girl's return. It is Catherine who suggests to the Emperor that "the best amends his majesty could make was to give her a handsome fortune and the colonel for a husband, who had the best right, having caught her in pursuit of his game."

Wordsworth is sparing in his details of Ina's return, having bent his main effort depicting her fortitude during the year of exile. In the conclusion he merely states that the Emperor, "heart-smitten by the wrong," sent a pledge to the maiden and gave a dower. Bruce is more explicit in detailing the Emperor's generosity:

> The czar . . . ordered one of his favourites to go with the colonel, and bring the young lady home. . . . The marriage was under the direction, and at the expense of the czar, who himself gave the bride to the bridegroom; saying, that he presented him with one of the most virtuous of women; and accompanied his declaration with very valuable presents, besides settling on her and her heirs, three thousand rubles a year.[27]

Bruce concludes his story with words similar to those used by Wordsworth in his note to the poem: "Besides the concurring reports of other people, I had this her story from her own mouth."

One might ask why Wordsworth was interested in this story, and could probably find an answer after analyzing the nature of the changes he made. Why, for instance, did Wordsworth extend Ina's flight from a mere walk of several miles into an escape requiring seven days to accomplish? And why did he emphasize the loneliness of her retreat, both in describing it and in having her guardians visit her only occasionally? (Remember, that in Bruce's account either the nurse or her daughter attended the fugitive every night.) Though the individual changes may seem slight in enumerating them, the total result is something quite different from Bruce's essentially narrative presentation. In its place we have a poem where emphasis is laid upon the main character's feelings, where those qualities that Wordsworth thought most worthy of representing are brought to the fore in the personality of his heroine. Ina, a child of low and humble origin, spurns an illicit love match, dwells instead in solitude, lives simply and close to nature, thinks about her home and her parents, and puts her trust in heaven. Observe how many of Wordsworth's favorite themes are stressed in this poem: besides the main emphasis upon patient endurance of misfortune, we find solitude and plain living, the triumph of principle over expediency, and the essential goodness of the common man.

The Idiot Boy is another experimental poem, like *The Complaint of a Forsaken Indian Woman,* in which Wordsworth treats primitive and rustic people. Here he is concerned with maternal love. He learned, either during his tour of the Alps or, as Beatty thinks, through reading Coxe's *Travels,* that, in the Alps idiots are considered a blessing to their families.[28] Coxe's comment regarding that belief is as follows:

It has been asserted also, that the people very much respect these idiots, and even consider them *as blessings* from Heaven. . . . For having . . . repeatedly inquired among the lower ranks, I am convinced, that the common people esteem them as blessings. They call them *"Souls of God, without sin":* and many parents prefer these idiot-children to those whose understandings are perfect; because, as they are incapable of intentional criminality, they consider them as certain of happiness in a future state. Nor is this opinion entirely without its good effect; as it disposes the parents to pay greater attention to such helpless beings.[29]

While the reader of a travel book, on coming across such a passage, might merely exclaim, "How curious and unusual!" Wordsworth does not dwell upon the love of the mother for her idiot son merely to amaze his readers. Though the treatment of this unfortunate creature had been called not "a fit subject for poetry," [30] Wordsworth took pains to explain why he thought it was. In answer to that charge, he wrote to John Wilson as follows:

I can only say that the loathing and disgust which many people have at the sight of an idiot, is a feeling which, though having some foundation in human nature, is not necessarily attached to it in any virtuous degree, but is owing in a great measure to a false delicacy, and, if I may say it without rudeness, a certain want of comprehensiveness of thinking and feeling. Persons in the lower classes of society have little or nothing of this: if an idiot is born in a poor man's house, it must be taken care of, and cannot be boarded out. . . . I have, indeed, often looked upon the conduct of fathers and mothers of the lower classes of society towards idiots as the great triumph of the human heart. It is there that we see the strength, disinterestedness, and grandeur of love; nor have I ever been able to contemplate an object that calls out so many excellent and virtuous sentiments without finding it hallowed thereby, and having something in me which bears down before it, like a deluge, every feeble sensation of disgust and aversion.[31]

It is to the last three sentences in this passage that we should pay particular attention, comparing them with Coxe's comment quoted above. This letter of Wordsworth's was written in 1802, two years after the famous preface to his second edition of *Lyrical Ballads* in which he expresses a preference for studying the lower classes of society in his attempt to depict "the essential passions of the heart." Coxe likewise explains why he is inclined to believe the statements of common people regarding the prevailing attitude towards idiots. Is it not likely that Wordsworth, at a time when he was in the process of formulating his own theories of man and nature, should supplement his personal experience with the observations of this explorer and traveler from whose writings he had already borrowed freely?

Of the poems in the edition of 1800, the one that most clearly shows the influence of Wordsworth's reading in travel books and, at the same time, reveals his interest in primitive and rustic people is *Ruth*. To line 64 of this poem Wordsworth appends the following note: "The splendid appearance of these scarlet flowers, which are scattered with such profusion over the hills in the southern parts of North America, is frequently mentioned by Bartram in his Travels." Following this clue, Dowden, Knight, Cooper, Lowes and others have uncovered borrowings from Bartram throughout the poem. Their findings, together with some comments of my own, will be briefly summarized here.

In the poem Wordsworth introduces a young man who relates his experiences among the Cherokee Indians in Georgia:

> There came a Youth from Georgia's shore—
> A military casque he wore,
> With splendid feathers drest;
> He brought them from the Cherokees;
> The feathers nodded in the breeze,
> And made a gallant crest.   (19-24)

Lowes remarks that: "The feathered casque in [this] stanza is an unmistakable reminiscence of Bartram's frontispiece." He also points out that "the strawberry gatherers in the ninth stanza are recalled from the graphic account of the strawberry beds in Bartram, p. 288." [32] Bartram's account follows:

> We . . . enjoyed a most enchanting view; a vast expanse of green meadows and strawberry fields . . . companies of young, innocent Cherokee virgins, some busy gathering the rich fragrant fruit, others having already filled their baskets, lay reclined under the shade . . . other parties, more gay and libertine, were yet collecting strawberries, or wantonly chasing their companions. [33]

From this passage Wordsworth apparently formed the ninth stanza of *Ruth*:

> He told of girls — a happy rout!
> Who quit their fold with dance and shout,
> Their pleasant Indian town,
> To gather strawberries all day long;

> Returning with a choral song
> When daylight is gone down.   (49-54)

The next two stanzas contain descriptions of flowers and trees:

> He spake of plants that hourly change
> Their blossoms, through a boundless range
> Of intermingling hues;
> With budding, fading, faded flowers
> They stand the wonder of the bowers
> From morn to evening dews.

> He told of the magnolia, spread
> High as a cloud, high over head!
> The cypress and her spire;
> —Of flowers that with one scarlet gleam
> Cover a hundred leagues, and seem
> To set the hills on fire.   (55-66)

Observe the similarity between these verses and the following description from Bartram:

Here is a species of Magnolia . . . it is a tall tree, sixty or eighty feet in height; the trunk is straight; its head terminating in the form of a sharp cone; the leaves are oblong. . . . The tall aspiring Gordonia lasianthus, which now stood in my view in all its splendour, is every way deserving of our admiration. Its thick foliage, of a dark green colour, is flowered over with large milk-white fragrant blossoms, [the leaves] are gradually changing colour, from green to golden yellow, from that to a scarlet, from scarlet to crimson; and lastly to a brownish purple. . . . So that the Gordonia lasianthus may be said to change and renew its garments every morning throughout the year.[34]

Lane Cooper thinks there is a more important relation between the thinking of Bartram and Wordsworth than the obvious similarity revealed by comparing certain passages in the two writers. In the *Athenaeum* he writes: "One may assume that Bartram's ideal (Introduction, pp. xxiv-xxv) of an essential, all-pervading moral intelligence 'which animates the inimitable machines' of nature, sufficiently approaches Wordsworth's 'moral life' in 'every natural form' to warrant a deeper study of Bartram." [35] In the main, we can accept this; and in our study of *The Prelude* we shall see that both Bartram and Wordsworth praised the American Indian as a noble savage. However, in the characterization of the degenerate hero in *Ruth* Wordsworth shows that an "ideal" environment is no positive guarantee of good behavior. Indeed, if the natural environment, however beautiful, is too luxuriant, it may contribute toward loose conduct and indolence. The young Englishman who marries and then deserts Ruth was brought up among savages in America; "a Youth from Georgia's shore," he was a true child of nature:

> With hues of genius on his cheek
> In finest tones the Youth could speak:
> —While he was yet a boy,
> The moon, the glory of the sun,
> And streams that murmur as they run,
> Had been his dearest joy. (31-6)

After describing his life among the Indians and the exotic foliage of the southern part of America, the youth depicts for Ruth the happy, carefree life they could lead there together.

> "Sweet Ruth! and could you go with me
> My helpmate in the woods to be,
> Our shed at night to rear;
> Or run, my own adopted bride,
> A sylvan huntress at my side,
> And drive the flying deer!" (91-6)

After their marriage Ruth looked forward eagerly to life in America on the "green savannahs." Unfortunately, however, she never got there, partly because of the influence of her husband's former companions with whom his boyhood had been spent:

> But ill he lived, much evil saw,
> With men to whom no better law
> Nor better life was known;
> Deliberately, and undeceived,
> Those wild men's vices he received,
> And gave them back his own·   (145-50)

This, combined with the luxurious and sensuous climate that had nourished him, overcame his genuine attempts to lead a nobler life. As a result, "once again he wished to live/ As lawless as before." In short, he deserts his wife and returns to America alone.

Now the interesting point about the characterization of this primitive is that, though his failure to behave decently and in conformity to the requirements of society, seems to be out of keeping with Wordsworth's beliefs, actually his behavior can be accounted for without refuting the poet's faith in the beneficient effects of a natural setting on man's moral and spiritual development. The youth's unsuccessful struggle against his lower and wilder impulses, so far as it is attributed to his environment, serves merely to define more specifically the kind of natural setting that Wordsworth thought ideal. For the near-tropical climate of southern America, though it nurtured this potentially noble character along with a host of beautiful flowers, was probably too lush to suit the more austere mood of the Lake Poet. Wordsworth admired the noble savage, not because he is loose living, indolent, and free from moral restraint, but because he is relieved of the "artificial" demands imposed by an unnatural society. He admired the sturdy Alpine hunter or the pioneer facing danger; but he was not sympathetic toward the indolence which probably characterizes some uncivilized peoples.

There is another point to consider in accounting for the character of Wordsworth's youth from Georgia's shore. We concluded our discussion of *The Complaint of a Forsaken Indian Woman* by observing that, though Wordsworth was faithful in the main to the details of Hearne's account, he had introduced into the characterization of the forsaken mother an emotional tone calculated to make his poem the vehicle for serene and tender thoughts. In *Ruth,* however, the plot requires that Wordsworth's primitive, while not utterly devoid of characteristics intended to arouse sympathy in the reader, be classed among the very few villains in the poet's galaxy of simple characters. For dramatic purposes, therefore, Wordsworth forgoes on this occasion his usual practice of idealizing his primitive and rustic characters.

In accounting for the source of this poem, Wordsworth states in the Fenwick note: "Written in Germany 1799. Suggested by an account I had of a wanderer in Somersetshire." Though this note would seem to settle the question of the poem's source, we are aware of Wordsworth's habit of combining first-hand experience, or incidents gained through talks with various characters, with his reading in travel books; consequently, we are not surprised to find in Bartram's *Travels,* if not an exact parallel to the behavior of Ruth's husband, something equally significant in suggesting to Wordsworth the type of wild, carefree child of nature that this character was to be. In the same chapter from Bartram in which are described the strawberry beds and the flowers, there is mention of a young trader who serves as Bartram's guide during part of the journey. The spectacle which he points out to Bartram of the Cherokee maidens gathering strawberries is commented on by the explorer:

The sylvan scene of primitive innocence was enchanting, and perhaps too enticing for hearty young men long to continue idle spectators.

In fine, nature prevailing over reason, we wished at least to have a more active part in their delicious sports. Thus precipitately resolving, we cautiously made our approaches, yet undiscovered, almost to the joyous scene of action. Now, although we meant no other than an innocent frolic with this gay assembly of hamadryades, we shall leave it to the person of feeling and sensibility to form an idea to what lengths our passions might have hurried us, thus warmed and excited, had it not been for the vigilance and care of some envious matrons who lay in ambush, and espying us, gave the alarm.[36]

This episode ends innocently enough with the white men eating strawberries "encircled by the whole assembly of the innocent jocose sylvan nymphs." There is, however, just enough suggestion of the free and easy relations existing between the traders and the Indian maidens to make it unlikely that Wordsworth, who followed so closely some of the other details, such as the happy, singing, dancing girls gathering strawberries, would have entirely overlooked the parallel between this young guide who might easily have been swept away by the lush and enticing surroundings, and the young Englishman, living far from home, in the wilds of America, where promiscuous standards of behavior prevailed.

In discussing *Descriptive Sketches,* we have shown that Wordsworth regarded the Swiss mountaineer as possessing some attributes of primitive man, and as living in surroundings calculated to develop the highest qualities in him. Another primitive type that Wordsworth admired perhaps as much as he did the Swiss was the American Indian. Whereas the poet learned about the Swiss partly through personal observation, partly through reading books like Coxe and Ramond, he must have learned about the Indian entirely from his wide reading in travel books. Indeed, it would be reasonable to assume that Wordsworth had never actually seen an Indian, except for a remark in the seventh book of *The Prelude,* in which he describes some of the spectacles that the city of London offers to the traveler:

> All moveables of wonder, from all parts,
> Are here—Albinos, painted Indians, Dwarfs . . .
> All out-o'-the-way, far-fetched, perverted things,
> All freaks of nature, all Promethean thoughts
> Of man . . .
> All jumbled up together, to compose
> A Parliament of Monsters.   (VII, 706-18)

The Indian is, in this instance, regarded merely as an oddity to be lumped together with dwarfs and other curiosities as a likely attraction in a freak show. On at least one other occasion, as we shall see in examining *The Excursion,* Wordsworth represents the Indian in an unfavorable light; but by and large he held the Indian in high esteem. Though as a young man recently graduated from Cambridge, he may have regarded him as a freak of nature, gazing upon him, as he tells us in *The Prelude,* with the curiosity of the sightseer in a strange metropolis, he was soon to discover in the Indian many admirable qualities that are often lacking in more highly civilized men. An examination of certain passages in *The Prelude* shows that Wordsworth associated the Indian with some of his most cherished concepts: with childhood, with simplicity, and with solitude.

In the idyllic picture that he paints of his own childhood, he compares his freedom and activity with that of an Indian:

> Oh! many a time have I, a five years' Child,
> A naked Boy, in one delightful Rill,
> A little Mill-race sever'd from his stream,
> Made one long bathing of a summer's day . . .
>   as if I had been born
> On Indian Plains, and from my Mother's hut
> Had run abroad in wantonness, to sport,
> A naked Savage, in the thunder shower.
>   (I, 291-304, 1805)

To the Indian is attributed also a child's naiveté and enthusiasm. Writing of "The pleasure gathered from the rudiments/ Of geometric science," (VI, 116-7) Wordsworth tells us that, as a young student, he approached the study "With Indian awe and wonder, ignorance pleased/ With its own struggles." (VI, 121-2)

In the conclusion to the seventh book, "Residence in London," Wordsworth compares the simplicity and dignity of the Indian with the plight of the city-dweller,

> Living amid the same perpetual whirl
> Of trivial objects, melted and reduced
> To one identity, by differences
> That have no law, no meaning, and no end.
>   (VII, 725-8)

Wordsworth felt that, because of his own boyhood surroundings, his

>   early converse with the works of God
> Among all regions; chiefly where appear
> Most obviously simplicity and power,   (VII, 742-4)

he could recognize what to the Londoner was meaningless confusion as parts of a unified whole, for,

> It is not wholly so to him who looks
> In steadiness, who hath among least things
> An under-sense of greatest; sees the parts
> As parts, but with a feeling of the whole.   (VII, 733-6)

Even with this advantage of understanding which he enjoyed over the city dweller, Wordsworth's early visit to London served mainly to strengthen his preference for the simplicity of country life. Yet in describing the contrast between city and country in *The Prelude,* he uses, not only the recollections of his own boyhood, but one striking passage which echoes his reading in travel books. After considering the city dweller, Wordsworth advises us to think of the noble savage:

> Think, how the everlasting streams and woods,
> Stretched and still stretching far and wide, exalt
> The roving Indian; on his desert sands,
> What grandeur not unfelt, what pregnant show
> Of beauty, meets the sun-burnt Arab's eye.   (VII, 745-9)

Wordsworth glorifies the freedom and spontaneity of the child; he also praises simplicity of life. With both these qualities he endows the American Indian. He also pictures the Indian as glorying in his solitude. In a passage of some 200 lines from the "Y" manuscript, never incorporated into the text of *The Prelude,* but bearing on "the growth of the poet's soul under the interacting influences of Nature and Man," Wordsworth pictures the devotee of nature contemplating civilization and depreciating it as made up of "sordid men," "transient occupations," "desires/ Ignoble and depraved."

> Therefore he cleaves
> Exclusively to Nature as in her
> Finding his image, what he has, what lacks,
> His rest and his perfection.

He is interested in "primary and independent life."

> Single he is in state, monarch and king;
> Or like an Indian, when, in solitude
> And individual glory, he looks out
> From some high eminence upon a tr(act)
> Boundless of unappropriated earth.[37]

How does one account for this preponderance of praise for the Indian, for this emphasis on the nobler elements of his character? In discussing the borrowings from Hearne, we commented on the poet's tendency to idealize everything he touched. That would account for the praise. The interest in the Indian as such stems in part from the vogue begun by Rousseau of celebrating the savage. But with Wordsworth the interest was, in its initial stages, more personal than literary; so far as we associate this interest with the poet's reading it may be regarded as an extension of his early preference for simple and rustic characters, such as the villagers with whom he struck up an acquaintance during his years at Hawkshead School. We recall his statement in *The Prelude*: "And Shepherds were the men that pleased me first" (VIII, 128). Given that interest, he might have turned back to the pastoral conventions of the shepherd type and celebrated in his poems the characters from the "Arcadian fastnesses," "the wild woods/ Of Arden," or "such as Spenser fabled." [38] But that would have run counter to his theory of poetry with its announced intention of keeping his reader "in the company of flesh and blood." Therefore, when he chose to supplement his first-hand knowledge of simple and rustic characters, he turned instead to straight-forward accounts of Swiss peasants, such as those described by Coxe and Ramond. Certainly Wordsworth was, by inclination, sympathetic toward the type of man living close to nature away from the artificialities of civilization so despised by Rousseau. He counted as one of the great blessings of his childhood the fact that his earliest concept of man had been a noble one. He had seen man first as simple and dignified, working against a background of natural grandeur. Such an experience could fortify him against possible disillusionment later in life when he came upon petty or ignoble men working amid surroundings destined to imbrute them. As he explains his recollection of shepherds in *The Prelude*:

> A rambling school-boy, thus
> I felt his presence in his own domain,
> As of a lord and master, or a power,
> Or genius, under Nature, under God,
> Presiding; and severest solitude
> Had more commanding looks when he was there. . . .
> Thus was man

75

Ennobled outwardly before my sight,
And thus my heart was early introduced
To an unconscious love and reverence
Of human nature; hence the human form
To me became an index of delight,
Of grace and honour, power and worthiness. . . .
> blessed be the God
Of Nature and of Man that this was so;
That men before my inexperienced eyes
Did first present themselves thus purified. . . .
> were it otherwise,
And we found evil fast as we find good
In our first years, or think that it is found,
How could the innocent heart bear up and live!
But doubly fortunate my lot. . . .
> that first I looked
At Man through objects that were great or fair;
First communed with him by their help.
> (VIII, 256-317)

Wordsworth felt the truth of this experience very strongly and wished to communicate it to his readers. Consequently, he must have welcomed as substantiating evidence of his faith the testimony found in the *Travels* of William Bartram, a Philadelphia Quaker and explorer. Bartram is full of praise for the Indian, arguing that, since the savage is untutored, his goodness is natural and part of the divine plan. Bartram writes:

Can it be denied, but that the moral principle, which directs the savages to virtuous and praiseworthy actions, is natural or innate? It is certain they have not the assistance of letters, or those means of education in the schools of philosophy, where the virtuous sentiments and actions of the most illustrious characters are recorded, and carefully laid before the youth of civilized nations: therefore this moral principle must be innate, or they must be under the immediate influence and guidance of a more divine and powerful preceptor, who, on these occasions, instantly inspires them, and as with a ray of divine light, points out to them at once the dignity, propriety, and beauty of virtue.[39]

Bartram's account contains descriptions of Indian settlements. Sometimes the descriptions are merely factual, such as the following:

> I suddenly saw before me an Indian settlement, or village. It was a fine situation, the bank rising gradually from the water. There were eight or ten habitations, in a row, or street, fronting the water, and about fifty yards distance from it. Some of the youth were naked, up to their hips in the water, fishing with rods and lines.[40]

Sometimes, however, he concludes a descriptive passage with a rhapsodic utterance. The following lines, for example, have been cited as the source for one of Wordsworth's poems:

> How happily situated is this retired spot of earth! What an elysium it is! where the wandering Siminole, the naked red warrior, roams at large, and after the vigorous chase retires from the scorching heat of the meridian sun. Here he reclines, and reposes . . . his verdant couch guarded by the Deity; Liberty, and the Muses, inspiring him with wisdom and valour, whilst the balmy zephyrs fan him to sleep.[41]

Lane Cooper believes that this passage inspired the following lines in *Stanzas written in My Pocket-Copy of Thomson's "Castle of Indolence"*:

> Retired in that sunshiny shade he lay;
> And, like a naked Indian, slept himself away.

May it not also account for certain phrases in Wordsworth's description of Indians in *The Prelude?* Though his superior poetic judgment generally leads him to a more restrained phraseology, it is not difficult to trace the similarity between such a passage from Bartram, and Wordsworth's descriptions. For example, in Bartram we have the "wandering Siminole" who "roams at large." In *The*

Prelude we find "the roving Indian." [42] Bartram describes the "naked red warrior" and the naked youth "fishing with rods and lines." Wordsworth writes of the "naked Savage." [43]

Perhaps even more significant than the similarities of expression is the similarity of attitude toward the Indian. Bartram was not blind to the Indian's faults; he occasionally represents him attacking and robbing white settlers; but he does not dwell upon the cruel, savage activity with which many Americans commonly associate the Indian. Since the object of his *Travels* was to glorify God or, as he tells us, since "my chief happiness consisted in tracing and admiring the infinite power, majesty, and perfection of the great Almighty Creator," [44] he was prone to find goodness in all God's creatures. It is significant that Wordsworth, who read several books depicting the Indian in a far less favorable light than did Bartram, saw eye to eye with the Quaker explorer. The inclination was already there in the poet's mind; it was strengthened and reaffirmed by the realistic account of this adventurer.

In tracing the influence of Bartram on Wordsworth, Lane Cooper has pointed out an important parallel indicative of Wordsworth's interest in primitivism. Among the poet's illustrations of a natural setting for man's activities, we find a description of the ideal university, situated, not at Cambridge, but in "a Virgin grove,/ Primaeval in its purity and depth." Cooper observed the similarities between Wordsworth's description in *The Prelude* and a passage from Bartram:

> Oh! what a joy it were
> To see a Sanctuary for our Country's Youth,
> With such a spirit in it as might be
> Protection for itself, a Virgin grove,
> Primaeval in its purity and depth. . . .
> A habitation sober and demure
> For ruminating creatures, a domain
> For quiet things to wander in, a haunt

> In which the Heron might delight to feed
> By the shy rivers, and the Pelican
> Upon the Cypress spire in lonely thought
> Might sit and sun himself.   (III, 439-54, 1805)

I ascended this beautiful river, on whose fruitful banks the generous and true sons of liberty securely dwell, fifty miles above the white settlements. . . . My progress was rendered delightful by the sylvan elegance of the groves, cheerful meadows, and high distant forests, which in grand order presented themselves to view. . . . Behold, on yon decayed, defoliated cypress tree, the solitary wood pelican, dejectedly perched upon its utmost elevated spire; he there, like an ancient venerable sage, sets himself up as a mark of derision, for the safety of his kindred tribes.[46]

Here we have the groves and a cypress tree with "the solitary wood pelican, dejectedly perched upon its utmost elevated spire." In Wordsworth we find "a Virgin grove" and "the Pelican/ Upon the cypress spire in lonely thought." For Bartram's "scenes of grandeur and sublimity," Wordsworth has "A habitation sober and demure," etc. Like the pantisocrats who dreamed of reestablishing the golden age along the banks of the Susquehanna, Wordsworth dreamed of establishing a college in this beautiful section of Georgia described by Bartram.

Bartram's is not, however, the only travel book used as source material for *The Prelude*. A few pages earlier we noted that, in making the distinction between city and country life, Wordsworth used a passage reminiscent of his reading in travel books to point the contrast between the Londoner and the Indian or Arab. Again in Book VIII he describes "the Paradise/ Where I was rear'd" as even lovelier than "Gehol's famous gardens."

> Beauteous the domain
> Where to the sense of beauty first my heart
> Was open'd, tract more exquisitely fair

> Than is that Paradise of ten thousand Trees,
> Or Gehol's famous Gardens, in a Clime
> Chosen from widest empire, for delight
> Of the Tartarian Dynasty . . .
> Scene link'd to scene, an evergrowing change,
> Soft, grand, or gay! . . .
>   Groves of foliage taught to melt
> Into each other their obsequious hues
> Going and gone again, in subtile chace,
> Too fine to be pursued; or standing forth
> In no discordant opposition, strong
> And gorgeous as the colours side by side
> Bedded among rich plumes of Tropic Birds;
> And mountains over all embracing all;
> And all the landscape endlessly enrich'd
> With waters running, falling, or asleep.
> But lovelier far than this the Paradise
> Where I was rear'd; in Nature's primitive gifts
> Favor'd no less.   (VIII, 119-46, 1805)

Wordsworth's source here, as de Selincourt's note indicates, was Lord Macartney's description quoted in John Barrow's *Travels in China*.[47] The gardens described in Barrow were artificial and were planned with the idea of making the view most effective from the various pleasure houses. "In particular spots . . . the views appeared to have been studied. The trees were not only placed according to their magnitudes, but the tints of their foliage seemed also to have been considered in the composition of the picture." (This description, incidentally, which appears a few pages before the passage cited by de Selincourt, bears a strong similarity to the lines from *The Prelude* quoted above beginning, "Groves of foliage taught to melt.") With all this careful planning the effect of wild nature was not entirely lacking. The banks of the river, for example, "are neither trimmed, nor shorn, nor sloped . . . but have been thrown up with immense labour in an irregular, and, as it were, fortuitous manner, so as to represent the free hand of nature."[48] Though

Wordsworth makes it clear that these are man-made scenes, so effective is their artificiality that he regards them as objects of natural beauty comparable to the familiar scenes of his boyhood; and he imagines the part they would play in that stage of a child's development when he grows unconsciously from love of nature to love of man.

> Yea, doubtless, at an age when but a glimpse
> Of those resplendent Gardens, with their frame
> Imperial, and elaborate ornaments,
> Would to a child be transport over-great,
> When but a half-hour's roam through such a place
> Would leave behind a dance of images
> That shall break in upon his sleep for weeks;
> Even then the common haunts of the green earth,
> With the ordinary human interests
> Which they embosom, all without regard
> As both may seem, are fastening on the heart
> Insensibly, each with the other's help,
> So that we love, not knowing that we love,
> And feel, not knowing whence our feeling comes.
> (VIII, 159-72, 1805)

There are two points to be observed here: first, the importance that Wordsworth attaches to a natural or primitive setting in developing the emotional life of the child; secondly, the fact that the most carefully landscaped gardens or parks can only approximate the pristine beauty of nature. As arduously as the gardeners had worked to imitate the wild effect of nature in Gehol's famous gardens, they could not, in Wordsworth's opinion, equal the truly primitive paradise in which he had been born. Macartney's account of these gardens does remind the poet of his own birthplace and of the transports of delight and the "dance of images" that such a scene of beauty would produce in the mind of the child. Yet, for all their charm, they fall short of true nature: "lovelier far than this the Paradise/ Where I was rear'd."

Whereas in this passage from *The Prelude* Wordsworth praises the gardens of Gehol because they approximate nature, in another poem he criticizes the garishly artificial embellishments surrounding an object of natural beauty. The setting of the poem, *Effusion in the Pleasure-ground on the Banks of the Bran, near Dunkeld,* is a waterfall and a theatrically arranged apartment near it. The scene is described in Dorothy's *Journal* of September 8, 1803. Although Dorothy's comment, most of which Wordsworth printed as a preface to his poem, contains no criticism of the inappropriateness and bad taste of so artificial a device in a setting of natural grandeur, her brother's poem points out man's folly in attempting such embellishment:

> O Nature—in thy changeful visions,
> Through all thy most abrupt transitions
> Smooth, graceful, tender, or sublime,
> Ever averse to pantomime—
> Thee neither do they know nor us
> Thy servants, who can trifle thus . . .
> Thus (where the intrusive Pile, ill-graced
> With baubles of theatric taste,
> O'erlooks the torrent breathing showers
> On motley bands of alien flowers
> In stiff confusion set or sown,
> Till Nature cannot find her own,
> Or keep a remnant of the sod
> Which Caledonian Heroes trod)
> I mused; and, thirsting for redress,
> Recoiled into the wilderness.
> (31-6, 119-28)

Commenting on this poem in the Fenwick note, Wordsworth remarks: "I am not aware that this condemnatory effusion was ever seen by the owner of the place. He might be disposed to pay little attention to it; but were it to prove otherwise, I should be glad, for the whole exhibition is distressingly puerile."

Was Wordsworth aware that his poetical protest was not the first objection to be lodged against this artificial display? In a book that Wordsworth knew well and had mentioned in a note to *The Excursion,* I, 341, Heron, after describing the cataract with the building hanging over it in much the same fashion as Dorothy did in her *Journal,* proceeds to criticize the theatrical effect produced by the room inlaid with mirrors, in a manner that might well have suggested the tone of the lines in Wordsworth's poem quoted above.

> The glaring gaiety of the room was of a character inconsistent with that of the objects around it [the river, waterfall, and rocks, which Heron has been praising]. It dispelled the solemn awe, and pleasing melancholy with which those impressed the mind . . . and the consequent effect was, that the imagination and the feelings were harassed and disgusted. . . . To add to this, the mirrours which are inlaid round the walls, and in the ceiling of this apartment, are, by a fantastic contrivance, so disposed, as to afford various reflections of the whitened volume of water, as it pours down the cataract; like smoke, like flame, like boiling oil. This is Conceit of which the contriver was probably very proud. . . . But, I must confess, that I could not help considering it with other sentiments than those of admiration.[49]

As we have observed in considering some of Wordsworth's other borrowings, the fact that he did not acknowledge any debt to Heron in this poem does not preclude the possibility of the poet's having borrowed from him here, as we know he did in *The Excursion.*

The Affliction of Margaret is another poem, like *Ruth* (see *supra,* pp. 70-1), in which Wordsworth's statement concerning its origin does not entirely settle the question of sources. In the Fenwick note he informs us that the main character in the poem was taken from among his acquaintances:

> This was taken from the case of a poor widow who lived in the town of Penrith. Her sorrow was well known to Mary, to my Sister,

and, I believe, to the whole town. She kept a shop, and when she saw a stranger passing by, she was in the habit of going out into the street to inquire of him after her son.

Margaret is characterized as a simple rustic character who despises "worldly grandeur" and "fortune with her gifts and lies." The son who is only briefly described, has, nevertheless, a parallel in a travel book that Wordsworth may have read. Coleridge's poem, *To a Young Lady*, contains the character Lee Boo, and the author's note reveals that he is taken from Keate's *Account of the Pelew Islands*. Aware of Coleridge's and Wordsworth's interest in travel literature at this time, Professor Cooper was not surprised to find two points of similarity between the "Anecdotes of Lee Boo" in *Pelew Islands* and *The Affliction of Margaret* as well as its overflow, *The For-saken*. First, the appearance and character of Lee Boo may have suggested to Wordsworth his description of Margaret's son:

> He was among the prime in worth,
> An object beauteous to behold;
> Well born, well bred; I sent him forth
> Ingenuous, innocent, and bold.

Lee Boo, whose portrait appears on page 364 of Keate's *Pelew Islands,* is described as having "a countenance so strongly marked with sensibility and good-humor, that it instantly prejudiced every-one in his favour . . . eyes so quick and intelligent." He is further characterized by the following phrases which are not unlike the description from Wordsworth quoted above: "ingenuous openness," "native simplicity," "courteous and pleasant," "natural good-breeding." [50] Cooper comments as follows on the possibility of Lee Boo's portrait having suggested to Wordsworth the description of Margaret's lost son:

Wordsworthians will readily bring to mind the connexion between the 'Youth from Georgia's shore' in 'Ruth' and the frontispiece, 'Mico

Chlucco, the Long Warrior, King of the Siminoles,' in Bartram's 'Travels.' It is not uncharacteristic of Wordsworth to fuse the lineaments or trappings of an aborigine in his projection of one who 'spake the English tongue.' [51]

In the second place, there is a marked similarity, as Cooper points out, between the anxiety of Lee Boo's father, who never learns that his son died of smallpox during his stay in England, and "the alternations of hope and fear in the afflicted Margaret."

> Seven years, alas! to have received
> No tidings of an only child;
> To have despaired, have hoped, believed,
> And been for evermore beguiled.

Compare these lines with the following phrases from Keate: "occasionally alarmed by doubt — yet still buoyed up by hope," "wearied out by that expectation . . . he had nourished in vain." *"Hope turned to Despair."* Note also the similarity between the following verses:

> Where art thou, my beloved Son,
> Where art thou, worse to me than dead?
> Oh find me, prosperous or undone!
> Or, if the grave be now thy bed,
> Why am I ignorant of the same
> That I may rest; and neither blame
> Nor sorrow may attend thy name?

and these lines from Keate: "As the human mind is far more pained by uncertainty than a knowledge of the worst — every reader will lament . . . [the boy's father] should to this moment remain ignorant, that his long-looked-for Son can return no more." [52] The influence of Keate is also evident in the following lines from *The Forsaken*:

I only pray to know the worst;
And wish, as if my heart would burst.
O weary struggle! silent years
Tell seemingly no doubtful tale . . .
                and fears
And hopes are strong and will prevail.

Another possible literary source for *The Affliction of Margaret,* heretofore unobserved by scholars, is to be found in de Saussure's *Voyages dans les Alpes,* a book cited by Beatty as a source for *Descriptive Sketches.*[53] The parallel is not close enough for one to say positively that Wordsworth has borrowed from de Saussure here, but the passages are of a type that would have attracted Wordsworth's notice as illustrating the beliefs of primitive and other superstitious people. The first passage, taken from the account of the chamois hunter mentioned by Beatty, describes the reluctance of the hunters' wives to sleep during their husbands' absence for fear that the ghost of a husband killed in the chase might appear in their dreams.

Ces chasseurs restent quelquefois ainsi plusieurs jours de suite dans ces solitudes, & pendant ce temps-là . . . leurs malheureuses femmes . . . sont livrées aux plus affreuses inquiétudes, elles n'osent pas même dormir dans la crainte de les voir paroître en songe; car c'est une opinion reçue dans le pays, que quand un homme a péri, ou dans les glaces, ou sur quelque rocher ignoré, il revient de nuit apparoître à la personne qui lui étoit la plus chère, pour lui dire où est son corps.

The second passage, from the same chapter, describes a widow whose father, husband, and brothers have died in an epidemic. She cannot understand why their ghosts have not returned to visit her.

"Mais ce qui est bien étrange, c'est que de tant qui s'en sont allés, il n'en soit pas revenu un seul: moi," ajouta-t-elle avec l'expression de la douleur, "qui ai tant regretté mon mari & mes frères, qui n'ai cessé de penser à eux, qui toutes les nuites les conjure avec les plus vives instances de me dire où ils sont, & dans quel état ils se trouvent: ah sûrement s'ils existoient quelque part, ils ne me laisseroient pas dans cette incertitude!" [55]

The last sentence in this passage recalls the plight of Margaret wavering between hope and despair, though with the difference that the woman in de Saussure's account is in doubt, not as to whether her relatives are alive or dead, but as to whether their souls exist in another world. Both passages seem quite similar to the ninth stanza of *The Affliction of Margaret*:

> I look for ghosts; but none will force
> Their way to me: 'tis falsely said
> That there was ever intercourse
> Between the living and the dead;
> For, surely, then I should have sight
> Of him I wait for day and night,
> With love and longings infinite.

So in *The Affliction of Margaret* we find another of the poems dealing with simple types in which a good deal of the expression, probably more than Wordsworth himself suspected, comes from travel books. Granted that he had known poor Margaret, just as he had seen idiots in his youth, the fact remains that this poem, as well as *The Idiot Boy,* draws heavily on literary sources.

It will be especially significant to discover evidences of primitivism in the Wanderer because there is in this Wordsworthian character so much, not only of the poet's autobiography, but also of his aspirations and ideals. According to Fausset,

The character at least of The Pedlar, or The Wanderer, as he was later called . . . was, in fact, the consummation of such characters as Wordsworth had dramatised in some of the *Lyrical Ballads.* Freed from domestic ties and the struggle for survival, he lacked the pathos

87

of those earlier figures. But he was the better qualified thereby to personify Wordsworth's ideal of the complete man and to be the voice of his mature convictions.[56]

In the account of The Wanderer's early life, Wordsworth restates a theme to which he had given expression earlier in his "Preface to the *Lyrical Ballads*"; namely, that in "Humble and rustic life . . . the essential passions of the heart find a better soil in which they can attain their maturity . . . speak a plainer and more emphatic language . . . and . . . are incorporated with the beautiful and permanent forms of nature." Professor Knight has called attention to the similarity between the above-mentioned passage from the *Preface* and the following lines in *The Excursion*: [57]

> From his native hills
> He wandered far; much did he see of men,
> Their manners, their enjoyments, and pursuits,
> Their passions and their feelings; chiefly those
> Essential and eternal in the heart,
> That, 'mid the simpler forms of rural life,
> Exist more simple in their elements,
> And speak a plainer language.   (I, 340-7)

The significant point for this study is that Wordsworth wrote a note to *The Excursion,* I, 341 stating that he had found his own opinion regarding the beneficent influence of nature on man sub-stantiated in the writings of a traveler well acquainted with Scotland. This is characteristic of the way in which Wordsworth draws upon the judgment of other writers to reaffirm or illustrate some of his most cherished convictions, in this instance his belief in primitivism. Wordsworth's note to *The Excursion* (edition of 1820) and the quotation from Heron follow:

At the risk of giving a shock to the prejudices of artificial society, I have ever been ready to pay homage to the aristocracy of nature;

under a conviction that vigorous human-heartedness is the constituent principle of true taste. It may still, however, be satisfactory to have prose testimony how far a Character, employed for purposes of imagination, is founded upon general fact. I, therefore, subjoin an extract from an author who had opportunities of being well acquainted with a class of men, from whom my own personal knowledge emboldened me to draw this portrait.

He then quotes the following passage from Heron's *Observations* of Scotland:

We learn from Caesar and other Roman writers, that the travelling merchants who frequented Gaul and other barbarous countries, either newly conquered by the Roman arms, or bordering on the Roman conquests, were ever the first to make the inhabitants of those countries familiarly acquainted with the Roman modes of life . . . and to enjoy Roman conveniences. In North America, travelling merchants from the settlements have done and continue to do much more towards civilizing the Indian natives, than all the Missionaries, Papist or Protestant, who have ever been sent among them. . . .

It is farther to be observed, for the credit of this most useful class of men, that they commonly contribute, by their personal manners no less than by the sale of their wares, to the refinement of the people among whom they travel. Their dealings form them to great quickness of wit, and acuteness of judgment. Having constant occasion to recommend themselves and their goods, they acquire habits of the most obliging attention, and the most insinuating address. As, in their peregrinations, they have opportunity of contemplating the manners of various men and various cities; they become eminently skilled in the knowledge of the world. *As they wander, each alone, through thinly-inhabited districts, they form habits of reflexion, and of sublime contemplation.* (Italics Wordsworth's.) With all these qualifications, no wonder, that they should often be, in remote parts of the country, the best mirrors of fashion, and censors of manners; and should contribute much to polish the roughness, and soften the rusticity of our peasantry. It is not more than twenty or thirty years, since a young man going from any part of Scotland to England, of purpose to *carry the pack,* was considered, as going to lead the life, and to acquire the fortune of a gentleman. When, after twenty years' absence, in that honourable line of employment, he returned, with his acquisitions tc his native country, he was regarded as a gentleman to all intents and purposes.[58]

When *The Excursion* was first published in 1814, Wordsworth appended the following shorter note to I, 341 because, as he explains, he did not at that time have Heron's book on hand:

> In Heron's Tour in Scotland is given an intelligent account of the qualities by which this class of men used to be, and still are in some degree, distinguished, and of the benefits which society derives from their labours. Among their characteristics, he does not omit to mention that, from being obliged to pass so much of their time in solitary wandering among rural objects, they frequently acquire meditative habits of mind, and are strongly disposed to enthusiasm poetical and religious. I regret that I have not the book at hand to quote the passage, as it is interesting on many accounts.[59]

When he later had access to the book and quoted from it, he omitted parts of the three paragraphs that bear closely on this part of *The Excursion*. In the first place, he omitted Heron's topic sentence: "I am induced to observe, that chapmen or pedlars, are the great civilizers of countries and nations." He also omitted the last sentence of the first of Heron's paragraphs, and all of the second paragraph which reads:

> Nothing can be more natural, than that these things should so happen. A rude people will hardly go in search of commodities of which they know not the names, the nature, or the value, and which they have little, if any money to purchase. Yet, when such commodities are brought among them, exposed to their view, and recommended as fashionable or useful; they seldom fail to take a fancy for them, and will often give in exchange any thing of however essential utility, that they already possess. They learn to labour, that they may have means with which to purchase those foreign commodities. — They learn to disdain the use of those coarse clothes, or rude utensils with which they

were before content. And with the new conveniences, they insensibly
adopt that improved system of manners to which such conveniences
properly correspond. In the stage of the progress of society in which
this change is begun, no such alteration could possibly take place,
without the intervention of chapmen or pedlars.

It seems to me that Wordsworth's praise of pedlars contained in
the lines,

> An irksome drudgery seems it to plod on,
> Through hot and dusty ways, or pelting storm,
> A vagrant Merchant under a heavy load
> Bent as he moves, and needing frequent rest;
> Yet do such travellers find their own delight;
> And their hard service, deemed debasing now,
> Gained merited respect in simpler times;
> When squire, and priest, and they who round them dwelt
> In rustic sequestration — all dependent
> Upon the PEDLAR'S toil — supplied their wants,
> Or pleased their fancies, with the wares he brought,
>
> (I, 322-32)

owes much to this passage from Heron which Wordsworth omitted
from his quotation, as well as to the part quoted by him. Note especially that Wordsworth seems to echo Heron's praise of the pedlar
as a civilizing influence. Compare the poetry quoted above with
these phrases from Heron: "Chapmen or pedlars are the great
civilizers of countries and nations . . . travelling merchants from
the settlements have done . . . much . . . toward civilizing the
Indian natives . . . no such alteration could possibly take place,
without the intervention of chapmen or pedlars." As we have seen
earlier in this study, when Wordsworth refers to a line of his poetry
as stemming from a certain passage in a travel book, evidence of
other unacknowledged borrowings can sometimes be found by
searching either in adjacent lines of his poetry or in other passages
in the travel book near the passage he has cited.

The pedlar who "gained merited respect in simpler times" may not seem to belong to Wordsworth's family of primitives and rustics. After all, he was fond of "the divine Milton" (*Excursion,* I, 250) and had taught a village school. Yet, in his out-of-doors, wandering life and in his service to the rural inhabitants, he displayed those qualities of the simple life which Wordsworth found and idealized in primitive and rustic people. It is significant to observe here that Wordsworth, with all his enthusiasm for primitive virtues, is impressed by the passage in Heron which represents pedlars as links between civilization and the more nearly primitive state. Note that Heron's description not only portrays the pedlars as bringing useful wares to the natives, but also points out that "they commonly contribute, by their personal manners . . . to the refinement of the people among whom they travel." All this seems to substantiate the point made earlier in this chapter that Wordsworth was interested in primitivism, not because he literally advocated a return to nature, but because he hoped to improve the particular civilization to which he belonged. The character of the Pedlar suggests, not only that civilized people can learn from observing the manners of simple and rustic people, but also that their more primitive neighbors can benefit from contact with them. In the development of a nation of warriors, the presence of merchants and pedlars might have a deleterious effect, if we can believe the familiar words of Caesar:

Horum omnium fortissimi sunt Belgae, propterea quod a cultu atque humanitate provinciae longissime absunt, minimeque ad eos mercatores saepe commeant atque ea quae ad effeminandos animos pertinent important.[60]

Yet Wordsworth's praise of the pedlar indicates that intercourse between rustics and the representatives of civilization in the person of the wandering pedlar could be mutually beneficial.

As for other borrowings in *The Excursion,* Fagin remarks in his chapter on "Bartram's Influence on Literature" that *The Excursion,* III, 915-43, owes much to Bartram's *Travels.* He is cautious in indicating the exact debt, pointing out that

Wordsworth had read many travel books picturing unpopulated American regions, and it is not wise to be definite as to which was the source of a particular passage in such an ambitious poem as *The Excursion.* It is more certain that frequently they all united in his mind to form a composite impression of America, so that it is not at all strange to find the Mississippi and the St. Lawrence ("that northern stream/ That spreads into successive seas") merged in the same passage. However, that a good deal of Bartram has crept into these lines is a not unreasonable hypothesis.[61]

Fagin further reasons that, since Wordsworth obviously took Bartram's "solitary wood pelican, dejectedly perched upon . . . [the cypress tree's] utmost elevated spire," for "the pelican/ Upon the cypress spire in lonely thought," he may very well have remembered the next paragraph in Bartram for his description in *The Excursion* of the "vast/ Expanse of unappropriated earth." The passage from Bartram cited by Fagin is as follows: "Thus secure and tranquil, and meditating on the marvellous scenes of primitive nature, as yet unmodified by the hand of man, I gently descended the peaceful stream, on whose polished surface were depicted the mutable shadows from its pensile banks." [62]

Fagin feels even more confident that there are borrowings from Bartram in Book IV of *The Excursion.* The following passage, for example,

> Here closed the Sage that eloquent harangue,
> Poured forth with fervour in continuous stream,
> Such as, remote, 'mid savage wilderness,
> An Indian Chief discharges from his breast
> Into the hearing of assembled tribes,
> In open circle seated round,   (IV, 1276-81)

he thinks may have come from either of the following two passages in Bartram: "We took our seats in a circle of venerable men, round a fire in the centre of the area . . . I was struck with awe and veneration at the appearance of a very aged man . . . the whole circle saluted him," or "The people being assembled and seated in order . . . the ball opens, first with a long harangue or oration, spoken by an aged chief. . . . This oration was delivered with great spirit and eloquence." [63] Note that the words *seated, circle, assembled, eloquent, harangue,* and *chief* in the two passages from Bartram also appear in Wordsworth's comparison.

To return to the concluding portion of Book Three, there are echoes from other travel books besides Bartram to be found in the following lines:

> "So, westward, tow'rd the unviolated woods
> I bent my way; and, roaming far and wide,
> Failed not to greet the merry Mocking-bird;
> And, while the melancholy Muccawiss
> (The sportive bird's companion in the grove)
> Repeated o'er and o'er his plaintive cry,
> I sympathised at leisure with the sound;
> But that pure archetype of human greatness,
> I found him not. There, in his stead, appeared
> A creature, squalid, vengeful, and impure;
> Remorseless, and submissive to no law
> But superstitious fear, and abject sloth."   (III, 944-55)

Professor Knight has pointed out that the "merry Mocking-bird" was probably taken from Thomas Ashe's *Travels in America,* and that the "Muccawiss," another name for whip-poor-will, came from Jonathan Carver's *Travels in North America.* [64] No one has ventured to suggest a definite source for the "creature, squalid, vengeful, and impure," whom the *Solitary* found in place of the expected "pure archetype of human greatness." Wordsworth's suggestion for this ugly savage must have come from his reading in Samuel Hearne's *Journey from Hudson's Bay to the Northern Ocean,* a book from which, as we have shown, he acknowledged his borrowings in a note to *The Complaint of a Forsaken Indian Woman.* Compare Wordsworth's characterization of

> A creature, squalid, vengeful, and impure;
> Remorseless, and submissive to no law
> But superstitious fear, and abject sloth,

with Hearne's descriptions of Indians. Note that the following passages, representative of many that could be extracted from Hearne, parallel Wordsworth's characterization in respect to appearance, cruelty, slothfulness, and superstitious nature. In appearance, they are

old and wrinkled, even before they are thirty . . . [with] a broad flat face, small eyes . . . a low forehead . . . a clumsy hooknose, a tawny hide . . . (p. 129) their heads are infested with vermin. . . . A scorbutic disorder, resembling the worst stage of the itch, consumptions, and fluxes, are their chief disorders. (p. 320)

As for their lack of humanity and their cruelty,

I never saw a set of people that possessed so little humanity, or that could view the distresses of their fellow-creatures with so little feeling and unconcern . . . (p. 99) their whole thoughts were immediately engaged in planning . . . how they might steal on the poor Esquimaux the ensuing night, and kill them all while asleep . . . when finding all the Esquimaux quiet in their tents, they . . . fell on the poor unsuspecting creatures . . . and began the bloody massacre. (pp. 175, 178)

Regarding their slothfulness,

False pretences for obtaining charity are so common among those people . . . that the Governor is frequently obliged to turn a deaf ear to many who apply for relief; for if he did not, he might give away the whole of the Company's goods, and by degrees all the Northern tribe would make a trade of begging.   (pp. 299-300)

Writing on their superstitions, Hearne twice dismisses them as "silly notions" (pp. 176, 327). On another occasion, he speaks of the victims of superstitious beliefs as "poor deluding and deluded people" (p. 231). Writing more seriously, he explains how superstitious fear can actually lead to death:

When these jugglers take a dislike to, and threaten a secret revenge on any person, it often proves fatal . . . as, from a firm belief that the conjurer has power over his life, he permits the very thoughts of it to prey on his spirits, till by degrees it brings on a disorder which puts an end to his existence: and sometimes a threat of this kind causes the death of a whole family; and that without any blood being shed, or the least apparent molestation being offered to any of the parties.   (p. 233)

Wordsworth's adaptation of these passages from Hearne is not characteristic of the poet who preferred, as we have shown, to use in his poetry the rhapsodic utterances of Bartram and other explorers in praise of savage life. Therefore, we cannot agree with Lane Cooper, who cites Wordsworth's characterization of the squalid creature as evidence of the poet's rejection of the "fallacy of the 'natural man.' " Cooper writes:

But against one fundamental tenet of Rousseau, a tenet that was accepted in some guise or other by nearly every one with whom the young English poet came in contact, Wordsworth decisively reacted. The fallacy of the 'natural man' his study of travels in the new world immediately showed to be unsound. To assume that as we approach more closely to the state of aboriginal men we discover a more and more perfect type of humanity, was, he knew, to fly in the face of observed data. He was aware what aboriginal tribes were actually like. They were in even worse case than the hopeless dwellers in the immense complexity of London — that 'monstrous ant-hill on the plain.' They were by no means superlatively good and happy.[65]

However much one might agree with the good sense of Professor Cooper's comment on the true state of natural man, it seems evident that Wordsworth is here using the squalid creature dramatically to depict the disillusioned and bitter mental state of the *Solitary*. That his studies in travel books occasionally opened his eyes to the ugly side of natural man there can be little doubt. In fact, the squalid creature of *The Excursion,* the young man in *Ruth,* and the harsh Indian custom related in *The Complaint of a Forsaken Indian Woman* could all be used as evidence to challenge the position taken in Aldous Huxley's essay, "Wordsworth in The Tropics." Huxley attempts to show that Wordsworth failed to recognize the harsh and savage aspects of nature.[66] Although Wordsworth was, in fact, well aware of that phase of nature, a consideration of the uses to which he put his reading, such as we have discussed in this chapter, suggests clearly that the attractive side of primitive man made a more important impression on the poet than did some of these realistic details mentioned by Hearne and others.

Throughout this thesis we have spoken of Wordsworth's finding his ideas and beliefs regarding the innate goodness of ordinary men reaffirmed in the literature of travel. So frequently does he make use of this kind of substantiation that one might conceive of Wordsworth as a poet "'in search of a mythology," to borrow an expression used by Wellek and Warren in their *Theory of Literature*. They mention the "myths" of progress, democracy, equality, and universal education. Admitting that the term is not easy to define in this sense, they suggest that "as men can't live by abstractions alone, they have to fill their voids by crude, extemporized, fragmentary myths (pictures of what might be or ought to be)."[67] One of Wordsworth's most highly cherished "abstractions" was plain living and high thinking. For his images and symbols of what

97

plain living and high thinking might be or ought to be, he seized upon the Swiss mountaineer and the American Indian, rustic or savage man living remote from towns. Such a metaphorical interpretation of Wordsworth's interest in primitivism would do much to obviate the necessity of worrying unduly over his logic and consistency in setting up the noble savage as an *actual* standard by which civilized society should model its behavior. Perhaps this interpretation might also help to dispel the worries of humanists like Irving Babbitt who, in "The Primitivism of Wordsworth," seems to have taken too literally Wordsworth's preference for children, savages, and other simple people.[68] Occasionally the poet made use of unfavorable descriptions and characterizations found in his reading, such as this one of the squalid creature, or that of the wild, undisciplined young man in *Ruth*. But in that rather substantial portion of his work which shows the influence of travel literature, these unpleasant aspects of primitive people do not predominate. Instead, as we have attempted to show throughout this chapter, Wordsworth used his primitives and rustics to illustrate such inspiring concepts as the golden age of man, the free and simple life of a Swiss canton, the maternal love of a savage mother for her child or of a rustic for her idiot son, the roving freedom and childlike spontaneity of the Indian whose life is contrasted favorably with that of the city dweller. All these descriptions and characterizations seem to be verbalizations of Wordsworth's cherished concept of plain living and high thinking; and in his reading of travel books Wordsworth found an important part of the idiom for which he was seeking.

SUMMARY

IN THE INTRODUCTION WE NOTED THAT SEVERAL SCHOLARS HAVE called attention to Wordsworth's habit of borrowing from travel books, but that the question of the full extent of this borrowing and of the influence travel books had on his poetry has not been made the subject of a book-length study. Also, among too many critics, the idea that Wordsworth was largely uninfluenced by books seems to persist.

Consequently, this book has treated both the extent and influence of Wordsworth's borrowing from travel books. Hitherto unnoticed borrowings have been discovered in the following poems: *The Affliction of Margaret, At Rome, The Black Stones of Iona, Descriptive Sketches, Effusion . . . on the Banks of the Bran, near Dunkeld, The Excursion, In due observance of an ancient rite, A Morning Exercise, The Prelude, The Russian Fugitive, Ruth,* and *The Solitary Reaper.* Authors of travel books in which new borrowings have been discovered include: Barrow, Bartram, Bruce, Burnet, Coxe, de Saussure, Hearne, Heron, Laborde, Martin, Ramond, and Waterton. (For full reference, see the Appendix, where Wordsworth's acknowledgements of his debt to travel books, together with my findings and those of others, are summarized.)

The following conclusions were reached: 1) that the influence of travel books is evident in many of Wordsworth's poems, from the earliest down to those written late in life, and including poems that seem to spring directly from personal observation; 2) that he used material in travel books to furnish him with incidents and characters, to clarify the complex imagery of his personal observation, and to support certain tenets of his poetical credo; 3) that the close similarity between his phraseology and that of the travel books from which he borrowed indicates that the common notion regarding his habit of composing extemporaneously while out walking needs modification; 4) that some of his favorite themes and cherished concepts are found in travel books; these include: love of simplicity and solitude, faith in the perfectibility of man, interest in strange customs, distrust of the complexities of civilization, and preference for the life of dalesmen, savages, and mountaineers.

Wordsworth could and did draw on his personal observation and experience to illustrate many of these cherished concepts; at times, however, he preferred to begin with experiences already recounted by explorers and travelers, modifying the essentially narrative material of his sources to achieve the emotional tone for which he was striving. In this way travel books furnished an idiom and a "mythology"; they gave concrete form to his abstractions. And it seems particularly appropriate that books which opened the eyes of readers to the wonders of the new world should have so inspired and influenced the poet who, in his most representative work, led the way in a new era of poetry.

APPENDIX

THE FOLLOWING LIST CONTAINS TITLES OF FORTY-FOUR POEMS IN which Wordsworth borrowed from travel books, together with the names of the books. Where he himself acknowledged his indebtedness, as was often his custom, the item is marked with an asterisk. Reference is also made in this bibliography to articles and notes which should help scholars desiring to examine various borrowings and their effect on the poems. The list does not include titles of travel books that Wordsworth may have read or referred to, except where evidence of definite borrowing of phrase or idea has been reasonably well established. With this qualification, the list aims at completeness.

Many of the items contained in this list are included in the notes to *Wordsworth's Poetical Works,* ed. Ernest de Selincourt and Helen Darbishire. 5 vols. Oxford, 1940-9. Where this is so, the reference is given in abbreviated form to the volume and page. For example, in item No. 1 the abbreviation is (I, 22); where a book other than de Selincourt's is referred to, as in item No. 4, the reference is given more fully.

An Evening Walk, 1793
1. *Clarke, James, *A survey of the Lakes of Cumberland, Westmorland, and Lancashire.* London, 1787. (I, 22)
2. *Gilpin, William, *Observations on several parts of Great Britain, particularly the High-lands of Scotland.* 2 vols. London, 1778. (I, 30)
3. Gray, Thomas, *Journal in the Lakes,* 1775. In *The Works of Thomas Gray,* ed. Edmund Gosse. 4 vols. New York, 1895. (I, 323)
4. Hutchinson, William, *Excursion to the Lakes.* London, 1776. (See Arthur Beatty, *Wordsworth: Representative Poems.* New

York, 1937, p. 19.)
5. West, Richard, *Guide to the Lakes.* London, 1779. (See Beatty, *op. cit.,* p. 12.)
Descriptive Sketches, 1793
6. Gilpin, William, *Observations on several parts of England, particularly the mountains and lakes of Cumberland and Westmorland.* 2 vols. London, 1786. (See Beatty, *op. cit.,* p. 38.)
7. *Ramond de Carbonnières, Louis F. E. (published anonymously) *Lettres de M. William Coxe à M. W. Melmoth sur l'état politique, civil, et naturel de la Suisse.* 2 vols. Paris, 1782 (I, 64, 68, 70.)
8. de Saussure, Horace B., *Voyages dans les Alpes, précedes d'un essai sur l'histoire naturelle des environs de Geneve.* 4 vols. Neuchâtel, 1779-96. (See Beatty, *op. cit.,* p. 57.)
The Complaint of a Forsaken Indian Woman, 1798
9. *Hearne, Samuel, *A journey from the Prince of Wales's fort in Hudson's bay, to the Northern Ocean.* London, 1795. (II, 40)
Expostulation and Reply and *The Tables Turned,* 1798
10. Bartram, William, *Travels through North and South Carolina, Georgia, East and West Florida.* Philadelphia, 1791. (See N. B. Fagin, *William Bartram, Interpreter of the American Landscape.* Baltimore, 1933, pp. 175-6.)
The Idiot Boy, 1798
11. Coxe, William, *Sketches of the natural, civil, and political state of Swisserland; in a series of letters to William Melmoth, esq.* London, 1779. (See Beatty, *op. cit.,* p. 224.)
Lines composed . . . above Tintern Abbey, 1798
12. Gilpin, William, *Observations on the River Wye, and several parts of South Wales, &c.* (3rd ed.) London, 1792. (see J. B. McNulty, "Wordsworth's Tour of the Wye: 1798," *MLN,* XL, 5; May, 1945, pp. 291-5.)
Hart-Leap Well, 1800
13. Clarke, *op. cit.* (See Beatty, *op. cit.,* pp. 358-9.)
Ruth, 1800
14. *Bartram, *op. cit.* (II, 510)
There was a Boy, 1800

15. Bartram, *op. cit.* (See Lane Cooper, *Methods and Aims in the Study of Literature.* Boston, 1915, p. 115.)

The Affliction of Margaret, 1807

16. Keate, George, *An account of the Pelew Islands.* London, 1789. (See Lane Cooper, "Wordsworth Sources, Bowles and Keate," *Athenaeum,* April 22, 1905, pp. 498-500.)

17. de Saussure, *op. cit.,* II, 150, 166. (See C. N. Coe, "A Source for Wordsworth's 'The Affliction of Margaret,' 57-63," *MLN,* LXVII, 1; January, 1952, p. 38.)

The Blind Highland Boy, 1807

18. *Dampier, William, *A new voyage round the world.* 3 vols. London, 1697. (III, 448)

I wandered lonely as a cloud, 1807

19. Bartram, *op. cit.* (See *The Travels of William Bartram,* ed. Mark Van Doren, introduction by J. L. Lowes, New York, 1940, p. 6.)

The Kitten and the Falling Leaves, 1807

20. Bartram, *op. cit.* (See Fagin, *op. cit.,* p. 174.)

She was a Phantom of Delight, 1807

21. Bartram, *op. cit.* (II, 506)

The Solitary Reaper, 1807

22. Heron, Robert, *Observations made in a journey through the western counties of Scotland.* 2 vols. Perth, 1793. (See C. N. Coe, "A Note on Wordsworth's 'The Solitary Reaper,'" *MLN,* LXIII,7; November, 1948, p. 493.)

23. *Wilkinson, Thomas, *Tours to the British mountains, with the descriptive poems of Lowther, and Emont Vale.* London, 1824. (Referred to by Wordsworth as "Tour in Scotland," and read by him in manuscript many years before it was published.) (III, 445)

Song at the Feast of Brougham Castle, 1807

24. *Nicolson, Joseph, and Burn, Richard, *The history and antiquities of the counties of Westmorland and Cumberland.* 2 vols. London, 1777. (II, 515-6)

To H. C. Six Years Old, 1807

25. *Carver, Jonathan, *Travels through the interior parts of North-America*. London, 1778. (I, 364)

Hofer, 1809

26. Bartram, *op. cit.* (See Fagin, *op. cit.*, p. 160.)

The Excursion, 1814

27. Ashe, Thomas, *Travels in America performed in 1806, for the purpose of exploring the rivers Alleghany, Monongahela, Ohio, and Mississippi*. London, 1808. (See *Wordsworth's Poetical Works,* ed. William Knight. 8 vols. London, 1896, V, 395.)

28. Bartram, *op. cit.* (See Fagin, *op. cit.*, pp. 160-3.)

29. Carver, *op. cit.* (See Knight, *op. cit.*, V, 140-1.)

30. Falkner, Thomas, *A description of Patagonia, and the adjoining parts of South America*. London, 1774. (See Knight, *op. cit.*, V, 393.)

31. Hearne, *op. cit.* (See C. N. Coe, "A Source for Wordsworth's 'Squalid Creature,'" *N&Q,* 195, 4; Feb. 18, 1950, pp. 76-7.)

32. *Heron, *op. cit.* (See Wordsworth's note to *The Excursion,* I, 341.)

33. Purchas, Samuel, *Pvrchas his Pilgrimage*. London, 1613. (See J. S. Lyon, *The Excursion A Study,* New Haven, 1950, p. 60; and E. K. Holmes, "Some Sources of Wordsworth's Passages on Mythology," *MLN,* LIV, 2; February, 1939, pp. 127-9.)

Address to my Infant Daughter, Dora, 1815

34. Bartram, *op. cit.* (See Fagin, *op. cit.*, pp. 173-4.)

In due observance of an ancient rite, 1815

35. Laborde, Alexander de, *A view of Spain; comprising a descriptive itinerary, of each province*. 5 vols. London, 1809. (See C. N. Coe, "Wordsworth's Debt to Laborde's *View of Spain,*" *MLN,* LXIV, 1; January, 1949, pp. 29-31.)

The Oak of Guernica, 1815

36. *Laborde, *op. cit.* (III, 136)

O'erweening Statesmen have full long relied, 1815

37. *Laborde, *op. cit.* (III, 138)

Stanzas Written in my Pocket-Copy of Thomson's "Castle of Indolence", 1815

38. Bartram, *op. cit.* (See Cooper, *Athenaeum,* April 22, 1905, p. 499.)

American Tradition, 1820

39. *Humboldt, Alexander, *Personal narrative of travels to the equinoctial regions of the New continent.* 7 vols. London, 1814-29 (III, 253, 507)

Return and *Seathwaite Chapel,* 1820

40. *Green, William, *The Tourist's new guide, containing a description of the lakes, mountains, and scenery, in Cumberland, Westmorland, and Lancashire.* 2 vols. London, 1819. (III, 508)

Aix-la-Chapelle, 1822

41. *Ramond de Carbonnières, Louis F. E., *Observations faites dans les Pyrénées, pour servir de suite à des observations sur les Alpes, insérées dans une traduction des lettres de W. Coxe, sur la Suisse.* Paris, 1789. (III, 470)

Desultory Stanzas, 1822

42. *Ebel, Johann G., *Manuel du voyageur en Suisse.* (Tr. de l'allemand. 4 éd. française) Paris, 1818. (III, 488-9)

43. *Ramond de Carbonnières, Louis F. E., *Lettres de M. William Coxe,* 1781. (III, 488)

Illustration: the Jung-frau and the Fall of the Rhine near Schaffhausen, 1822

44. *Ibid.* (III, 568)

The Town of Schwytz, 1822

45. *Ebel, *op. cit.,* (III, 177)

Effusion in the Pleasure-ground on the Banks of the Bran, near Dunkeld, 1827

46. Heron, *op. cit.,* I, 171-2. (See C. N. Coe, "A Source for Wordsworth's 'Effusion,' " *N&Q,* 196, 4; February 17, 1951, pp. 80-1.)

The Pillar of Trajan, 1827

47. *Forsyth, Joseph, *Remarks on antiquities, arts, and letters, during an excursion in Italy.* London, 1813. (III, 502; see

also C. N. Coe, "A Note on Wordsworth's 'Pillar of Trajan,' "
N&Q, 197, 7; March 29, 1952, pp. 142-3.)

A Morning Exercise, 1832

48. *Waterton, Charles, *Wanderings in South America, the North-west of the United States, and the Antilles.* London, 1825. (II, 124; see also C. N. Coe, "A Note on Wordsworth's 'A Morning Exercise,' 1-18," *MLN,* LXIV, 1; January, 1949, pp. 36-7.)

The Black Stones of Iona, 1835

49. *Martin, Martin, *A description of the Western islands of Scotland.* London, 1703. (IV, 43; see also C. N. Coe, "A Source for Wordsworth's Sonnet, 'The Black Stones of Iona,' " *MLN* LXVI, 2; February, 1951, p. 102.)

The Egyptian Maid, 1835

50. Herbert, Thomas, *A relation of some yeares travaile, begunne Anno 1626. into Afrique and the greater Asia.* London, 1634. (III, 502.)

Hart's-horn Tree, 1835

51. *Nicolson, and Burn, *op. cit.* (III, 534-5)

The Russian Fugitive, 1835

52. *Bruce, Peter Henry, *Memoirs of Peter Henry Bruce. . . . Containing an account of his Travels in Germany, Russia, Tartary, Turkey, the West Indies, &c.* London, 1782. (IV, 441; see also C. N. Coe, "Wordsworth's 'The Russian Fugitive,' " *MLN,* LXIV, 1; January, 1949, pp. 31-6.)

Stanzas suggested in a Steamboat off Saint Bees' Heads, 1835

53. Bartram, *op. cit.* (See Cooper, *Athenaeum,* April 22, 1905, p. 500.)

At Rome, 1842 ("Is this, ye Gods, the Capitolian Hill?")

54. Burnet, Gilbert, *Travels through France, Italy, Germany, and Switzerland.* London, 1750. (See C. N. Coe, "A Source for Wordsworth's Sonnet, 'At Rome,' " *N&Q,* 193, 20; October 2, 1948, pp. 430-1.)

The Borderers, 1842

55. Bartram, *op. cit.* (See Fagin, *op. cit.,* p. 150.)

The Forsaken, 1842

56. Keate, *op. cit.* (See Cooper, *Athenaeum,* April 22, 1905, p. 498.)

The Prelude, 1850

57. Barrow, John, *Travels in China.* London, 1804. (See *Wordsworth's Prelude,* ed. Ernest de Selincourt. London, 1926, p. 550.)

58. Bartram, *op. cit.,* (See Cooper, *Athenaeum,* April 22, 1905, p. 499.)

59. Dampier, *op. cit.* (See *Wordsworth's Prelude,* ed. de Selincourt, p. 604.)

60. Haies, Edward, *A report of the voyage . . . attempted in . . . 1583 by Sir Humfrey Gilbert.* In Hakluyt's *Voyages.* London, 1589, III, 184-203 (ed. of 1809-12). (See *ibid.,* pp. 602-3.)

61. Hakluyt, Richard, *The principall navigations, voiages, and discoveries of the English nation.* London, 1589. (See *ibid.,* p. 504.)

62. Newton, John, *An authentic narrative of some remarkable and interesting particulars in the life of the Rev. Mr. John Newton.* London, 1764. (See R. D. Havens, *The Mind of a Poet.* Baltimore, 1941, pp. 412-3.)

63. *Park, Mungo, *Travels in the interior districts of Africa.* London, 1799. (See *Wordsworth's Prelude,* ed. de Selincourt, p. 603, l. 80. Park is mentioned, not by name, but as "that Land Traveller, living yet.")

64. Purchas, *op. cit.* (See *ibid.,* p. 544.)

NOTES

Notes on Introduction, pp. 11-22

1. Lane Cooper, *Methods and Aims in the Study of Literature*. Boston, 1915, pp. 96-8.
2. Emile Legouis, "William Wordsworth," *CHEL*, 15 vols. New York, 1907-33, XI, 104.
3. George McLean Harper, *William Wordsworth, His Life, Works, and Influence*. 2 vols. New York, 1916, I, 127.
4. *Wordsworth's Prelude*, ed. Ernest de Selincourt. Oxford, 1926, pp. xxviii-ix.
5. Thomas Stearns Eliot, *The Use of Poetry and the Use of Criticism*. Cambridge, Mass., 1933, p. 61.
6. Christopher Wordsworth, *Memoirs of William Wordsworth*. 2 vols. London, 1851, i, 10.
7. Quotations from *The Prelude* are taken from de Selincourt's edition. When the quotations are from the edition of 1805-6, as in this case, the date 1805 will follow the book and line reference; when no date follows this reference, the published edition of 1850 is referred to.
8. *The Early Letters of William and Dorothy Wordsworth*, ed. de Selincourt. Oxford, 1935, p. 155.
9. *Ibid.*, p. 188.
10. *The Poetical Works of William Wordsworth*, ed. Ernest de Selincourt and Helen Darbishire. 5 vols. Oxford, 1940-9, II, 474. (Much of the quoted matter in his book, including all the excerpts from Wordsworth's poems and most of the poet's notes, can be found in this edition. Where this is so, no footnotes have been considered necessary.)
11. *The Letters of William and Dorothy Wordsworth; the Middle Years*. ed. de Selincourt. 2 vols. Oxford, 1937, p. 487.

12. *Wordsworth's Prelude,* ed. de Selincourt, p. 544.
13. *Wordsworth's Poetical Works,* ed. de Selincourt, V, 373.
14. *The Letters of William and Dorothy Wordsworth; the Later Years.* ed. de Selincourt, 3 vols. Oxford, 1939, pp. 729, 773.
15. *Wordsworth's Poetical Works,* ed. de Selincourt, III, 489.
16. *Ibid.,* V, 373.
17. *The Prose Works of William Wordsworth,* ed. Alexander B. Grosart. 3 vols. London, 1876, III, 7, 159, 167, 38, 45.
18. See *Wordsworth's Prelude,* ed. de Selincourt, p. 500.
19. See Grosart, *op. cit.,* III, 435.
20. *Wordsworth's Prelude,* ed. de Selincourt, pp. xlii-iii.
21. *The Journals of Dorothy Wordsworth,* ed. de Selincourt. 2 vols. New York, 1941, I, 69-70, 102.
22. Alexander de Laborde, *A View of Spain.* 5 vols. London, 1809, II, 385.
23. J. G. Ebel, *Manuel du Voyageur en Suisse.* (4 éd. française) Paris, 1818, p. 509.

Notes on Chapter One, pp. 23-41

1. "Preface to the Second Edition of *Lyrical Ballads.*" (In this chapter, except where Wordsworth's notes refer to a particular poem, quotation from his theory of poetry are from this preface, the "Advertisement to the *Lyrical Ballads, 1798,*" or the "Essay, Supplementary to the Preface." See *Wordsworth's Poetical Works,* ed. de Selincourt, II, 383-430.)
2. *Wordsworth's Prelude,* ed. de Selincourt, p. 595.
3. See Raymond D. Havens, *The Mind of a Poet.* Baltimore, 1941, pp. 406, 426.
4. Gilbert, Burnet, *Travels through France, Italy, Germany, and Switzerland.* London, 1750, p. 231.
5. *Wordsworth's Poetical Works,* ed. de Selincourt, II, 507.
6. *The Journals of Dorothy Wordsworth,* ed. de Selincourt, I, 131-2.
7. For the interpretation of *I Wandered Lonely as a Cloud* contained in this paragraph, I am indebted to Professor Frederick A. Pottle, who suggested this idea to me while reading a

draft of my dissertation. He later elaborated on it in one of his lectures. See "The Eye and the Object in the Poetry of Wordsworth," *Wordsworth Centenary Studies*. Princeton, 1951, pp. 25 ff.

8. *The Travels of William Bartram,* ed. Mark Van Doren, intro. by J. L. Lowes. New York, 1940, p. 278.

9. *The Journals of Dorothy Wordsworth,* ed. de Selincourt, I, 380.

10. *Poems in Two Volumes, 1807,* ed. Helen Darbishire. Oxford, 1914, p. 336.

11. Robert Heron, *Observations made in a journey through . . . Scotland.* 2 vols. Perth, 1793, I, 286.

12. Havens, *op. cit.,* p. 27, n. 19.

13. *Wordsworth's Guide to the Lakes, fifth edition (1835),* ed. de Selincourt. London, 1906, p. 39.

14. Jonathan Carver, *Travels through the interior parts of North America.* London, 1778, pp. 132-3.

15. S. T. Coleridge. Quoted in *Wordsworth's Poetical Works,* ed. de Selincourt, III, 448.

16. *The Poetical Works of William Wordsworth,* ed. William Knight. 8 vols. London, 1896, V. 140.

17. Charles Waterton, *Wanderings in South America.* London, 1825, pp. 16-7.

18. *Ibid.,* pp. 141-2.

19. Havens, *op. cit.,* p. 62.

20. See Wordsworth's remarks on *Resolution and Independence* in C. Wordsworth's *Memoirs of William Wordsworth,* I, 173.

21. Quoted in Ernest Bernbaum, *Guide through the Romantic Movement.* 2nd ed. New York, 1949, p. 218.

Notes on Chapter Two, pp. 43-98

1. Havens, *op. cit.,* p. 351.

2. Arthur O. Lovejoy and George Boas, *A Documentary History of Primitivism and Related Ideas.* Baltimore, 1935, I, 1, 7-8.

3. Irving Babbitt, *Rousseau and Romanticism.* Boston, 1919, pp. 395 ff.

4. Hoxie N. Fairchild, *The Noble Savage.* New York, 1928, p. 180.

5. Hugh I'Anson Fausset, *The Lost Leader: A Study of Wordsworth.* London, 1933, p. 19.

6. *Ibid.,* p. 32.

7. *Ibid.,* p. 107.

8. *Wordsworth: Representative Poems,* ed. Arthur Beatty. New York, 1937, p. 34.

9. *Early Letters,* pp. 31-3.

10. William Coxe, *Sketches of the natural, civil, and political state of Swisserland.* London, 1779, I, 9-10 (ed. of 1789).

11. Coleridge. Quoted in Bernbaum, *op. cit.,* p. 32.

12. Henry David Thoreau, *Walden: or Life in the Woods.* Boston, 1854, Chap. II.

13. *Later Years,* pp. 56-7.

14. See Grosart, *op. cit.,* I, 10-1.

15. Quoted in Edith Batho, *The Later Wordsworth.* Cambridge, 1933, p. 126.

16. Batho, *op. cit.,* pp. 126, 140-1.

17. Beatty, *op. cit.,* pp. 36-61; Emile Legouis, *The Early Life of Wordsworth.* Tr. by J. W. Matthews, New York, 1932, pp. 475-7.

18. Coxe, *op. cit.,* I, 38-9. (Beatty, *op. cit.,* p. 55, n. 59, identifies this passage from Coxe as the source of *Descriptive Sketches,* 11. 539-40.)

19. *Ibid.,* I, 44-5.

20. Louis F. E. Ramond de Carbonnières, *Lettres de M. William Coxe . . . sur . . . la Suisse . . . augmentées des observations faites dans le même pays.* 2 vols. Paris, 1782, I, 80-1.

21. Lovejoy and Boas, *op. cit.,* I, 9.

22. Beatty, *op. cit.,* pp. 49-50, n. 42.

23. John Livingston Lowes, *The Road to Xanada.* Boston, 1927, p. 215.

24. Samuel Hearne, *A journey from . . . Hudson's Bay to the Northern Ocean.* London, 1795, ed. J. B. Tyrrell, Toronto,

The Champlain Society, 1911, pp. 218-9. (According to de Selincourt, *Wordsworth's Poetical Works,* II, 474-5, Edward Dowden identified this passage as a source for the poem.)

25. See *Wordsworth's Poetical Works,* ed. de Selincourt, II, 475.
26. Peter Henry Bruce, *Memoirs of Peter Henry Bruce.* London, 1782, p. 91.
27. *Ibid.,* pp. 93-4.
28. Beatty, *op. cit.,* pp. 224-5.
29. Coxe, *op. cit.,* I, 354-5.
30. By John Wilson in an appreciative letter on the *Lyrical Ballads;* see *Early Letters,* pp. 292, n. 2; 294.
31. *Early Letters,* pp. 296-7.
32. Lowes. In introduction to Bartram, *op. cit.,* p. 6.
33. Bartram, *op. cit.,* pp. 288-9.
34. *Ibid.,* p. 146.
35. Cooper, "Wordsworth Sources, Bowles and Keate," *Athenaeum,* April 22, 1905, p. 499.
36. Bartram, *op. cit.,* p. 289.
37. *Wordsworth's Prelude,* ed. de Selincourt, pp. 551, 558.
38. *Ibid.,* VIII, 133, 138-9, 144.
39. Bartram, *op. cit.,* pp. 45-6.
40. *Ibid.,* pp. 95-6.
41. *Ibid.,* p. 107. (See Cooper, *Athenaeum,* April 22, 1905, pp. 499.)
42. *Wordsworth's Prelude,* ed. de Selincourt, VII, 747.
43. *Ibid.,* I, 304, (1805).
44. Bartram, *op. cit.,* p. 82.
45. Cooper. See *Athenaeum,* April 22, 1905, p. 499.
46. Bartram, *op. cit.,* pp. 64-5.
47. *Wordsworth's Prelude,* ed. de Selincourt, p. 550.
48. John Barrow, *Travels in China.* London, 1804, p. 123.
49. Heron, *op. cit.,* I, 171-2.
50. George Keate, *An Account of the Pelew Islands.* London, 1789, pp. 366-73.
51. Cooper, *Athenaeum,* April 22, 1905, p. 498.

52. Keate, *op. cit.*, pp. 392-3.
53. Beatty, *op. cit.*, p. 57, n. 63.
54. Horace B. de Saussure, *Voyages dans les Alpes*. 4 vols. Neuchâtel, 1779-96, II, 150.
55. *Ibid.*, II, 166.
56. Fausset, *op. cit.*, p. 307.
57. Knight, *op. cit.*, V, 43.
58. Heron, *op. cit.*, I, 89-91.
59. Knight, *op. cit.*, V, 383.
60. Caesar, *De Bello Gallico*, I, i.
61. N. B. Fagin, *William Bartram, Interpreter of the American Landscape*. Baltimore, 1933, p. 161.
62. Bartram, *op. cit.*, p. 65.
63. *Ibid.*, pp. 391-2, 298. (See Fagin, *op. cit.*, p. 163.)
64. Knight, *op. cit.*, V, 140-1, 393 ff.
65. Cooper, *Methods and Aims in the Study of Literature*, p. 130.
66. Aldous Huxley, "Wordsworth in the Tropics," *Yale Review*, xviii (1929), pp. 672-83.
67. René Wellek and Austin Warren, *Theory of Literature*. New York, 1948, p. 197.
68. Irving Babbitt, "The Primitivism of Wordsworth," *The Bookman* (U.S.A.), lxxiv (1931), pp. 1-10.

BIBLIOGRAPHY

Ashe, Thomas, *Travels in America*. London, 1808.

Babbitt, Irving, *Rousseau and Romanticism*. Boston, 1919.

—"The Primitivism of Wordsworth, *"The Bookman* (USA), lxxiv (1931), pp. 1-10.

Barrow, John, *Travels in China*. London, 1804.

Bartram, William, *Travels through North and South Carolina, Georgia, East and West Florida*. Philadelphia, 1791.

Batho, Edith C., *The Later Wordsworth*. Cambridge, 1933.

Bernbaum, Ernest, *Guide through the Romantic Movement*. 2nd edition. New York, 1949.

Bruce, Peter Henry, *Memoirs of Peter Henry Bruce*. London, 1782.

Burnet, Gilbert, *Travels through France, Italy, Germany, and Switzerland*. London, 1750.

Caesar, C. Julius, *Caesar's Commentaries on the Gallic War*, ed. Albert Harkness. New York, 1901.

Carver, Jonathan, *Travels through the interior parts of North America*. London, 1778.

Clarke, James, *A Survey of the Lakes of Cumberland, Westmorland, and Lancashire*. London, 1787.

Cooper, Lane, *Methods and Aims in the Study of Literature*. Boston, 1915.

—"Wordsworth Sources, Bowles and Keate," *Athenaeum*, April 22, 1905, pp. 498-500.

Coxe, William, *Sketches of the natural, civil, and political state of Swisserland*. London, 1779.

Dampier, William, *A new voyage round the world*. 3 vols. London, 1697.

Dunklin, Gilbert T., *Wordsworth Centenary Studies*, ed. G. T. Dunklin. Princeton, 1951.

Ebel, Johann G., *Manuel du voyageur en Suisse*. Traduit de l'allemand. 4 éd. française . . . Paris, 1818.

Eliot, Thomas S., *The Use of Poetry and the Use of Criticism*. Cambridge, Mass., 1933.

Fagin, Nathan B., *William Bartram, Interpreter of the American Landscape*. Baltimore, 1933.

Fairchild, Hoxie N., *The Noble Savage*. New York, 1928.

Falkner, Thomas, *A description of Patagonia, and the adjoining parts of South America*. London, 1774.

Fausset, Hugh I'A., *The Lost Leader: A Study of Wordsworth*. London, 1933.

Forsyth, Joseph, *Remarks on antiquities, arts, and letters, during an excursion in Italy*. London, 1813.

Gilpin, William, *Observations on the River Wye, and several parts of South Wales, etc.* (3rd. ed.) London, 1792.

—*Observations on several parts of England, particularly the mountains and lakes of Cumberland and Westmorland*. 2 vols. London, 1786.

—*Observations on several parts of Great Britain, particularly the High-lands of Scotland*. 2 vols. London, 1778.

Gray, Thomas, *The Works of Thomas Gray*, ed. Edmund Gosse. 4 vols. New York, 1895.

Green, William, *The Tourist's new guide, containing a description of the lakes, mountains, and scenery, in Cumberland, Westmorland, and Lancashire*. 2 vols. London, 1819.

Haies, Edward, *A report of the voyage . . . by Sir Humfrey Gilbert*. In *Hakluyt's Voyages*. London, ed. of 1809-12, vol. 3.

Hakluyt, Richard. *The principall navigations, voiages, and discoveries of the English nation*. London, 1589.

Harper, George McLean, *William Wordsworth, His Life, Works, and Influence*. 2 vols. New York, 1916.

Havens, Raymond D., *The Mind of a Poet*. Baltimore, 1941.

Hearne, Samuel, *A journey from the Prince of Wales's fort in Hudson's bay, to the Northern Ocean*. London, 1795.

Herbert, Thomas, *A relation of some yeares travaile, begvnne Anno 1626*. London, 1634.

Heron, Robert, *Observations made in a journey through the western counties of Scotland*. 2 vols. Perth, 1793.

Holmes, Elisabeth K., "Some Sources of Wordsworth's Passages on Mythology," *Modern Language Notes,* LIV, 2; February, 1939, pp. 127-9.

Humboldt, Alexander, *Personal narrative of travels to the equinoctial regions of the New continent.* 7 vols. London, 1814-29.

Hutchinson, William, *Excursion to the Lakes.* London, 1776.

Huxley, Aldous, "Wordsworth in the Tropics," *Yale Review,* xviii (1929), pp. 672-83.

Jeffrey, Francis, "Poems in Two Volumes by William Wordsworth," (a review) *Edinburgh Review,* October, 1807, xxi, pp. 214-31.

Keate, George, *An account of the Pelew islands.* London, 1789.

Laborde, Alexander de, *A view of Spain.* 5 vols. London, 1809.

Legouis, Emile, *The Early Life of William Wordsworth.* Translated by J. W. Matthews. New York, 1932.

—"William Wordsworth," *The Cambridge History of English Literature,* ed. A. W. Ward and A. R. Waller. 15 vols. New York, 1907-33, xi, 103-28.

Lienemann, Kurt, *Die Belesenheit von William Wordsworth,* Berlin, 1908.

Lovejoy, Arthur O. and Boas, George, *A Documentary History of Primitivism and Related Ideas.* Baltimore, 1935.

Lowes, John L., *The Road to Xanadu.* Boston, 1927.

Lyon, Judson S., *The Excursion: a Study.* New Haven, 1950.

McNulty, J. Bard, "Wordsworth's *Tour of the Wye*: 1798," *Modern Language Notes,* XL, 5; May, 1945, pp. 291-5.

Martin, Martin, *A description of the Western islands of Scotland.* London, 1703.

Newton, John, *An authentic narrative.* 4th. ed., London, 1775.

Nicolson, Joseph and Burn, Richard, *The history and antiquities of the counties of Westmorland and Cumberland.* 2 vols. London, 1777.

Park, Mungo, *Travels in the interior districts of Africa.* London, 1799.

Pottle, F. A., "The Eye and the Object in the Poetry of Wordsworth," *Wordsworth Centenary Studies*. Princeton, 1951, pp. 23-42.

Purchas, Samuel, *Pvrchas his Pilgrimage*. London, 1613.

Ramond de Carbonnières, Louis, F. E., *Lettres de M. William Coxe à M. W. Melmoth, sur l'état politique, civil, et naturel de la Suisse . . . augmentées des observations faites dans le même pays*. 2 vols. Paris, 1782.

—*Observations faites dans les Pyrénées*. Paris, 1789.

de Saussure, Horace B., *Voyages dans les Alpes*. 4 vols. Neuchâtel, 1779-96.

Thoreau, Henry D., *Walden, or Life in the Woods*. Boston, 1854.

Waterton, Charles, *Wanderings in South America*. London, 1825.

Wellek, René and Warren, Austin, *Theory of Literature*. New York, 1948.

West, Richard, *Guide to the Lakes*. London, 1779.

Wilkinson, Thomas, *Tours to the British mountains*. London, 1824.

Wordsworth, Christopher, *Memoirs of William Wordsworth*. 2 vols. London, 1851.

Wordsworth, Dorothy, *The Journals of Dorothy Wordsworth*, ed. Ernest de Selincourt. 2 vols. New York, 1941.

Wordsworth, William, *Letters of the Wordsworth Family from 1787 to 1855*, ed. William Knight. Boston, 1907.

—*Poems in Two Volumes*, 1807, ed. Helen Darbishire. Oxford, 1914.

—*The Letters of William and Dorothy Wordsworth*, ed. Ernest de Selincourt. 6 vols. Oxford, 1935-39.

—*The Poetical Works of William Wordsworth*, ed. William Knight. 8 vols. London, 1896.

—*The Poetical Works of William Wordsworth*, ed. Ernest de Selincourt and Helen Darbishire. 5 vols. Oxford, 1940-49.

—*The Prelude, or Growth of a Poet's Mind*, ed. Ernest de Selincourt, Oxford, 1926.

—*The Prose Works of William Wordsworth*, ed. Alexander B. Grosart. 3 vols. London, 1876.

—*Wordsworth: Representative Poems,* ed. Arthur Beatty. New York, 1937.

—*Wordsworth's Guide to the Lakes, fifth ed. (1835)*, ed. Ernest de Selincourt. London, 1906.

INDEX

121